MW00654982

50 MOST IMPORTANT

THEOLOGICAL

TERMS

50 MOST IMPORTANT THEOLOGICAL TERMS

J. BRIAN TUCKER
DAVID FINKBEINER

MOODY PUBLISHERS
CHICAGO

© 2021 by
J. BRIAN TUCKER AND DAVID FINKBEINER

All rights reserved. No part of this book may be reproduced in any form without permission in writing from the publisher, except in the case of brief quotations embodied in critical articles or reviews.

All Scripture quotations, unless otherwise indicated, are taken from the Holy Bible, New International Version®, NIV®. Copyright ©1973, 1978, 1984, 2011 by Biblica, Inc.™ Used by permission of Zondervan. All rights reserved worldwide. www.zondervan.com The "NIV" and "New International Version" are trademarks registered in the United States Patent and Trademark Office by Biblica, Inc.™

Scripture quotations marked (ESV) are from the ESV® Bible (The Holy Bible, English Standard Version®), copyright © 2001 by Crossway, a publishing ministry of Good News Publishers. Used by permission. All rights reserved.

Scripture quotations marked NASB are taken from the New American Standard Bible®, Copyright © 1960, 1971, 1977, 1995, 2020 by The Lockman Foundation. Used by permission. All rights reserved. www.lockman.org

Scripture quotations marked CSB have been taken from the Christian Standard Bible®, Copyright © 2017 by Holman Bible Publishers. Used by permission. Christian Standard Bible® and CSB® are federally registered trademarks of Holman Bible Publishers.

Scripture quotations marked (NLT) are taken from the Holy Bible, New Living Translation, copyright ©1996, 2004, 2015 by Tyndale House Foundation. Used by permission of Tyndale House Publishers, Carol Stream, Illinois 60188. All rights reserved.

Scripture quotations marked KJV are from the King James Version.

Interior Design: Ragont Design
Cover Design: Kaylee Lockenour

Library of Congress Cataloging-in-Publication Data

Names: Tucker, J. Brian, author. | Finkbeiner, David, 1936- author.
Title: 50 most important theological terms / J. Brian Tucker, David Finkbeiner.
Other titles: Fifty most important theological terms
Description: Chicago : Moody Publishers, [2021] | Includes index. | Summary: "Theology can be intimidating, full of big words and lofty ideas. Yet theological terms aren't just for academicians. These powerful words belong to everyday Christians, too. The authors offer clear explanations of key terms from Bible doctrine. Beyond mere explanations, the authors help the reader understand why these terms matter"-- Provided by publisher.
Identifiers: LCCN 2021021158 | ISBN 9780802422606 (paperback) | ISBN 9780802499400 (ebook)
Subjects: LCSH: Theology, Doctrinal--Popular works. | Bible--Theology. | BISAC: RELIGION / Christian Theology / General | RELIGION / Biblical Reference / Handbooks
Classification: LCC BT77 .T79 2021 | DDC 230.03--dc23
LC record available at https://lccn.loc.gov/2021021158

Originally delivered by fleets of horse-drawn wagons, the affordable paperbacks from D. L. Moody's publishing house resourced the church and served everyday people. Now, after more than 125 years of publishing and ministry, Moody Publishers' mission remains the same— even if our delivery systems have changed a bit. For more information on other books (and resources) created from a biblical perspective, go to www.moodypublishers.com or write to:

Moody Publishers
820 N. LaSalle Boulevard
Chicago, IL 60610

1 3 5 7 9 10 8 6 4 2

Printed in the United States of America

To Brian's grandfather,
the Rev. Boyd K. Denham (1913–1983),
who was a wonderful example of a faithful pastor
and practical theologian.

and

to Dave's father,
Mr. Albert H. Finkbeiner (1929–2015),
who instilled in his family a love for his Savior
and for God's Word.

CONTENTS

9. THE DOCTRINE OF THE CHURCH (ECCLESIOLOGY)

10. THE DOCTRINE OF THE LAST THINGS (ESCHATOLOGY)

INTRODUCTION
How to Use This Book

Theology is a word that comes to us through the combination of two Greek terms, *theos* ("God") and *logos* ("word" or "study"). So, it can be described as words about God or, better yet, the study of God. It is a set of practices all Christians should be involved in, so as to better grasp the words God has revealed in Scripture, along with what He has revealed about Himself in the world around us. Theology is a human undertaking that should be practiced together with other believers in a spirit of faith, grace, love, worship, and open-minded humility (Acts 17:11; Rom. 12:1–5; Phil. 1:27; 1 Thess. 5:21; 2 Tim. 2:25). Studying theology helps us learn more about God, ourselves, and what is required of those who follow Him. Reading this book will assist you in this knowledge-based obedience by giving you clear definitions and suggested practices to help you embody your Christian identity as set forth in Scripture.

This book seeks to present the fifty most important theological terms. For those of us who teach theology regularly, trying to narrow it down to 50 is a tall order. Nevertheless, we did our best to present a list of terms critical for understanding important doctrines of the faith. No doubt other theologians would change our list in various ways, dropping some of the terms we explore and adding others we have not included. But this list represents our judgment call of what constitutes the fifty most important terms—sort of.

In truth, we did not limit our discussion to fifty theological terms. We actually deal with many more. It is unavoidable. Doctrines of the faith are intricately connected with one another; you cannot isolate them. For example, you can hardly talk about Christ's atoning work on the cross without also talking about terms like "penal substitution," "limited atonement," "propitiation," or even "descent into hell." This means that our fifty most important terms often function as larger categories under which other related terms appear. So, yes, we could have called the book something like: *50 of the Most Important Theological Terms—Plus a Lot More Related to Them*. But that would be too long and clunky.

Our fifty key terms are not listed in alphabetical order. Instead, we organized them into ten chapters. Each chapter represents one of the main areas of Christian doctrine. For example, chapter 4 deals with the doctrine of Christ, so we address five important theological terms pertaining to Christ in that chapter. Although this book represents a collaboration between both of us, we did divide the chapters between us. Dave wrote chapters 2, 4, 5, 8, and 10, and Brian wrote chapters 1, 3, 6, 7, and 9.

Given the nature of this book, readers can use it in at

least three ways. First, they can consult it as a reference work, something akin to a theological dictionary. If they come across a theological term they find confusing or unfamiliar, they can look up what it means here. And again, the list is not limited to the fifty most important ones; lots of other terms are explained in this book. To that end, we have included an index of theological terms at the end of the book to aid anyone looking for the meaning of a specific term.

Second, readers can use the book to survey a specific doctrine of the faith. Someone wanting a survey of the doctrine of salvation, for example, can read chapter 8. The terms discussed in each chapter flow together in order to provide an overview of the doctrine covered.

Third, readers can read all the chapters together to survey all the major doctrines of the Christian faith.

We pray that this book is useful in whatever way you choose to use it.

1

THEOLOGICAL PRACTICE AND IDENTITY
(Theological Prolegomenon)

 Theological Hermeneutics

Why do some people believe that you can lose your salvation while others say, "Once saved, always saved"? The answer is hermeneutics. Why do some people baptize infants while others only baptize believers? You guessed it—hermeneutics. Why do some churches allow women pastors while others do not? You know the drill by now—hermeneutics. Hermeneutics is the starting point for our theology. What we do here determines the kind of theological system that develops. Get your hermeneutical practices right, and you have a great chance to develop sound theology. So, what is theological hermeneutics?

Processes associated with understanding and interpreting the Bible, its historical culture, and its contemporary readers—along with various theological texts written to explain them—constitute the primary focus of theological hermeneutics. Hermeneutics, more broadly, builds on a Greek noun *hermēneutēs*, which in context may signify a person who engages certain interpretive processes to help another understand the significance of words (1 Cor. 14:28). An associated Greek verb, *hermēnuō*, highlights the processes associated with helping a person uncover the meaning and application of a group of texts (Luke 24:27). The lexical setting of these two words suggests the goal of hermeneutics: to draw out the original meaning (*exegesis*) along with its application (*contextualization*).

Theological hermeneutics also recognizes the role of the interpreter—sometimes this is called "exegeting the exegete." An interpreter's background plays an important part in the interpretive process. It is essential to reflect on and make explicit this location throughout the interpretive journey, so that this and other presuppositions are seen as welcomed guests and not invisible tricksters leading away from the goal of virtuous reading. A couple of these socio-theological locations will be discussed later in this chapter.

One important method, the *literal-grammatical-historical*, serves as a primary means for uncovering the author's intended meaning of Scripture by those whose socio-theological location is dispensationalism. In this approach, the interpreter focuses on the plain meaning of words in their context; he or she seeks to uncover the human author's intent by paying attention to the text's grammar, syntax, and genre. Words, phrases, clauses, and sentences are read in a "normal" or literal manner in order to uncover the theological message the author intended.

The historical context and the background of the Bible's message is also an important part of this process, since Scripture was written over thousands of years to people in diverse cultures in the Ancient Near East, Jewish, and Greco-Roman worlds. Paying attention to genre helps us discern the way the text communicates its message through guidelines specific to various literary types (e.g., law, narrative, poetry, letters, prophecy). Thus, the goal of the literal-grammatical-historical method is to help readers understand the original message in its original context. It is sometimes described as finding an answer to a simple question: "What did it mean?" It is important to ask that question before a reader pushes forward and asks the contemporary question: "What does it mean to me?" A helpful maxim to remember is that the Bible can't mean to us what it couldn't have meant to them. This will help navigate debates over the contemporary theological significance of Scripture.

Though the term "hermeneutics" often appears in books and articles without any further discussion, it is a crossroads for various theological systems. It is vital, then, to discern the hermeneutical approach an author presupposes and practices in their writing. For example, an author who claims Israel and the church are distinct in God's plan presupposes a literal-grammatical-historical method, while one who claims the church is the new Israel likely does not.

There are complex reasons for choosing one theological hermeneutical method over another, and it should be noted that there is significant overlap between these differing approaches. In this case, though, a prior commitment to the hermeneutics of covenant theology—and the role of, say, typology, the application of earlier literary forms to later texts—provides the basis for understanding the church as the new Israel. In this way, the literal-historical-grammatical method has been revised and may now be described as *redemptive-historical-grammatical.*

This approach recognizes an inherent weakness in the literal-historical-grammatical method: it is ill-equipped to explain the full meaning of the whole Bible. The overarching redemptive message of the Scriptures can get lost in the atomistic readings of the literal approach. Even though the literal-historical-grammatical approach acknowledges the progress of revelation, its focus on the *human* author's intent fails to account fully for the Holy Spirit's agency as the primary author of Scripture. This theological-hermeneutical crossroad will have massive implications in the way theologians put together their Bible (e.g., the fulfillment of prophetic passages such as Daniel 9:24–27 and Hosea 3:5).

Despite the differences between these two hermeneutical approaches, they generally share a commitment to the authority, inspiration, and inerrancy of Scripture (see **The Characteristics of Scripture**). However, another hermeneutical approach should be noted: the *historical-critical method.* Whereas the literal-historical and redemptive-historical approaches find patterns of meaningfulness internal to the Scriptures, the historical-critical method finds it primarily outside of the Bible.

The locus of authority belongs to the wider academic fields and adjunct disciplines. Generally, when armchair theologians come across claims that set aside the historic teaching of the church, reject the reality of miracles, or account for biblical details via natural explanations, a historical-critical hermeneutic is being used. This doesn't mean that this method must be jettisoned fully. When it is shorn of its naturalistic presuppositions (e.g., a denial of miracles), it can yield historical insights that inform theological readings of the Bible and provide bridges of empathy toward larger concerns raised in a contemporary context.

Others find the historical-critical method an unacceptable dialogue partner. The *theological interpretation of Scripture approach* takes an inward focus for interpretation and draws exclusively on the canon (see **Canon of Scripture**) and the creeds of the church as a way to understand the meaning of the Bible. This approach has much to commend it, and given the presuppositions of both the literal-historical-grammatical and the redemptive-historical-grammatical methods, both may be labeled as types of theological interpretation of Scripture.

 **Evangelical**

Are you an evangelical? It's complicated. I thought I was until someone told me that since I was, I was also a white supremacist. This is what happens when theological terms are defined by the broader culture. So let's clarify what it means.

"Evangelical" is a contemporary grouping of Protestant Christians that have their roots in late eighteenth- and early nineteenth-century revivalism. They generally share four characteristics, the well-known Bebbington Quadrilateral: biblicism (the centrality of the Bible), conversionism (the individual acceptance of Jesus as Savior), activism (the requirement for evangelism and mission), and crucicentrism (the atoning work of Jesus on the cross). While some of these characteristics may be shared with other Christian traditions, evangelicals are also further located in the context of the twentieth-century debates between theological liberals and conservatives. These three ideas—Protestant Christianity, revivalism, and Bebbington's Quadrilateral—triangulate the social identity of evangelicals in the United States today. The term is not used the same way in other parts of the world. In Europe, for example, it refers to an ecclesial identity that is not Roman Catholic. In the UK, it shares some similarities with the use in mainland Europe; however, it is also used as a subgroup identity for low-church Anglicans, as well as for those not attached to the Church of England but still identified by the above three ideas. This suggests that "evangelical" is not simply a political identity, as it is all too often presented in the early twenty-first century, though it is a contested and somewhat malleable term.

The term "evangelical" draws from the lexical setting of the New Testament Greek noun *euangelion*, which can have a contextual meaning such as "good news" or, as some English translations of the Bible translate it, "gospel" (Gal. 1:11; Rom. 1:1, 16). The rationale for this group label is that those committed to biblicism, conversionism, activism, and crucicentrism may properly be understood as those who have aligned their patterns of belief and embodiment with the aims of the gospel. It is the message that God has acted in Jesus of Nazareth in order to redeem humanity, establish the kingdom, and restore creation. The ecclesial communities who identify themselves as evangelical understand their mission as the proclamation of this good news throughout the world. While there is significant debate as to the social implications of the gospel, there is agreement on the centrality of Jesus to the message.

When the diverse ecclesial label "evangelical" is attached to the term "theology," it raises a perennial challenge: How does one define *evangelical theology*? It is a theology that has its focus on the gospel of Jesus Christ from beginning to end. Several implications may be detected from this. Evangelical theology is fully Trinitarian, orthodox in its Christological teaching, and animated both by Christ's atoning work on the cross and by the centrality of the Christian community of faith, gathered for worship and mission.

Two terms mentioned in the opening sentence of this entry need further definition: (a) Protestantism and (b) revivalism, since evangelicalism is a nested social identity within these two movements from church history. *Protestantism* · is a sixteenth-century movement of protest concerning the beliefs and practices of the Roman Catholic Church, itself a branch of Christendom that resulted from an earlier split with the Orthodox Church in 1054. The *material* principle of the Protestant Reformation—what made it possible—is that justification of sinners occurs by grace alone through faith alone in Christ alone. The *formal* principle—its unique shape—is Scripture alone. Scripture formed the doctrine that made possible a movement to reform the church for the glory of God alone. Since a protest movement is inherently unstable, though, Protestantism quickly branched into four streams: Lutheran, Reformed, Anglican, and Anabaptist. As these grew, further movements developed: Baptists, Methodists, and eventually Pentecostals.

The second movement important for understanding evangelicalism is *revivalism*, a conversion-and-renewal movement in the late eighteenth and early nineteenth centuries. Its roots were in the Reformation's Lutheran stream in Germany that developed into *pietism*—an approach to the Christian life emphasizing holiness and personal experience in contrast to the dry orthodoxy that had overtaken much of Europe. A shared spiritual ethos also developed with Puritanism, especially in England and America, along with the Great Awakening and eventually the Pentecostal outpourings. Revivalism was characterized by (a) longing for repentance, (b) confident expectation for revival, (c) gospel proclamation, and (d) renewal of ardor and scripturally based worship and mission practices.

Why does this matter? In the last several years, there has

been a move to give up on the "evangelical" label, with some referring to themselves as "ex-evangelicals." It has also, no doubt, been co-opted by political leaders and has drifted from its original gospel orientation. Labels matter, though, and sometimes we need to revisit what they indicate. When my evangelical identity reconnects the gospel with my theology and the church, it is functioning the way it should. But when it only connects an inward-focused subgroup, a condition referred to as *koinonitis*, then an intervention is needed—one that requires more than Dr. Phil.

3 Calvinism

Theologians refer to Calvinism in several different ways. It can indicate the specific teachings of John Calvin (1509–64), though that use is probably too narrow. It can also describe the views of his immediate followers as they sought to organize his views; while more accurate than the previous category, this is still too limited. It can also function as a metonym for Reformed or covenant theology. Generally, Calvinism is abridged by the use of the acrostic TULIP: total depravity, unconditional election, limited atonement, irresistible grace, and perseverance of the saints. These are later formulations that represent closely the type of Calvinism that emerged from the Synod of Dort (1618–19).

While it is popular to highlight TULIP as the prototype of Calvinism, it is more precisely understood as a particular response to *Arminianism*, or the five articles of Remonstrance put forth by those who aligned themselves with the teachings of Jacobus Arminius (1560–1609). While not as well known as TULIP, one recent summary of the five articles built on the acrostic ACURA: all are sinful, conditional election, unlimited atonement, resistible grace, and assurance of salvation. These five phrases are a close approximation of the Arminians' concerns with the theology of the Dutch Reformed Church in their 1610 debates. So, while TULIP may be helpful as a way to remember the doctrines of grace, it will not do as a taxonomic definition for Calvinism.

Calvinism is broader than the "five points" of TULIP. It is a diverse theological tradition whose encompassing logic allows for several streams within its confessional standards, some of which do not map precisely onto TULIP, though they remain within its orbit. This suggests that Reformed theology and Calvinism do not have the same boundaries. In the United States, the "new Calvinists" are those who identify with the five points. Some of these continue to identify as Baptists, identifying with Charles Spurgeon or other Puritan divines. A Calvinist minister may also lead a nondenominational congregation, drawing from TULIP but holding to a truncated Reformed doctrine of the church and the sacraments. These would all be Calvinist but not altogether Reformed.

What are the boundaries for *Reformed theology*? Theologians offer a consistent set of answers. First, their churches trace their roots to the sixteenth-century magisterial Reformers, rather than to the later seventeenth-century radical Reformers who are the genealogical descendants of Baptists and other nondenominational churches. Second, Reformed churches allow Scripture to serve as its "norming norm," with the various creeds and confessions functioning in a secondary way. These would include the Heidelberg Catechism, the Canons of the Synod of Dort, and the Westminster Confession. Third, the ecclesial identity of those embracing fully Reformed theology will organize their churches via Presbyterian and Episcopal church-polity structures. They will not be nondenominational or congregational. Fourth, a sacramental approach to ministry will mark Reformed theology, so the Lord's Supper and baptism will be seen as means of grace and not mere memorials or public testimonies. So, being Reformed and being a Calvinist are not the same thing. A Calvinist emphasizes TULIP, though not necessarily Reformed ecclesiology. Calvinism, then, is a bounded set of doctrinal emphases with a variety of ecclesiological expressions.

A recent example of this diversity is evangelical Calvinism, a loosely affiliated group of interpreters who have misgivings regarding the federal or orthodox understanding of Calvinism. This divergent form of Calvinism finds fruitful dialogue partners in Thomas and James Torrance as they function as interpreters of Karl Barth. Evangelical Calvinism is not to be confused with the new Calvinism, which is popular among younger evangelicals who espouse Reformed soteriology via the five points from Dort and who are disaffected with dispensationalism. This broad grouping of evangelicals includes those with differing eschatological views as well as those with differing positions on whether the miraculous spiritual gifts (see **Spiritual Gifts**) continue today. There are also diverse views among this group in regard to believer or infant baptism (see **Baptism**). This eclecticism, however, does not typically extend to dispensationalism.

4 Dispensationalism

When did you first discover the joy of being uncool? For some of us it was when we blew out the candles on our eighteenth . . . no, wait, our twenty-ninth . . . okay, maybe our forty-ninth birthday cake. Once we free ourselves from the desire to be accepted or part of the "in crowd," it allows us to orient our lives in a way that doesn't depend on what the cool kids or adults think. When it comes to theology, dispensationalism suffers from a lack of the cool factor; a lot of people raised in churches that teach it are looking to blow out the candles on this so-called naïve way to read Scripture. Often, though, they're rejecting a caricature of the hermeneutical and theological system, not a clear understanding of it. So, let's clarify what it is before we blow out the candles.

Dispensationalism is a set of hermeneutical processes practiced by some evangelical Protestants beginning in the late nineteenth and early twentieth centuries but continuing into the twenty-first century. One of its presuppositions is a rejection of *supersessionism*, an interpretive position that maintains the church has fulfilled or replaced Israel in God's plan. A corollary of this stance is that Israel and the church are distinct (see **Israel and the Church**). These concepts are evident in Scripture through the consistent application of the literal-historical-grammatical approach to hermeneutics.

Dispensationalism is also a philosophy of history, in that everything in history is oriented toward God's glory as He administers the affairs of the world in stages. The word "dispensation" comes from the Greek word *oikonomia* and can also be translated as "administration" or "economy." God administers the affairs of the world through promises, commandments, and principles by which to live. If humans fail to abide by these, judgment occurs, and the next stage of God's plan in the world emerges. While there is debate as to the number of these dispensations, seven are most common: innocence, conscience, human government, promise, law, grace/church, and kingdom/millennium.

Dispensationalism is the most distinctive approach to hermeneutics to survive from nineteenth-century revivalist evangelicalism. It can be traced back to the theology of John Nelson Darby and the Plymouth Brethren in mid-nineteenth century Britain. Popularized by Bible prophecy conferences, it evidenced the innovative position that ethnic Israel remains God's chosen people. In light of this, Israel will be restored in an earthly millennial kingdom so that all of God's promises to the nation will be fulfilled in a literal, not a figurative or spiritual, way.

Dispensationalism also highlights two shared theological positions: premillennialism and a pretribulation rapture (see **The Millennium** and **The Rapture**). The unique teaching on the church, history, and the last things has led to warm debates between dispensationalists and covenant theologians. *Covenant theology* is also a set of hermeneutical processes practiced by some evangelicals, though its practitioners draw from writings of sixteenth-century Reformers such as Ulrich Zwingli and Heinrich Bullinger. It is central to Reformed theology and Calvinism. Its interpretation of Scripture revolves around the presence of a covenant of works, redemption, and grace rather than the seven distinct dispensations. It relies on creedal and confessional statements, though in a subordinate way to Scripture, which functions as the "norming norm" among Presbyterian and Reformed churches. In covenant theology, the church is seen in continuity with the people of God in the Old Testament and becomes the new Israel in the New Testament. In regard to eschatology, rather than dispensational premillennialism, the dominant position is amillennialism (see **The Millennium**).

There are several crucial points of distinction between dispensationalism and covenant theology, but the use of typology functions as one of the more important ones. In dispensationalism, the covenantal promises made to Israel are not seen as types; they are continuing promises that will be fulfilled literally in the future. A corollary is that dispensationalists believe the author's intention, as evidenced by the grammar and syntax of an Old Testament passage, is not overridden by the Emmaus Road hermeneutic, where a New Testament passage is thought to provide new, Christocentric meaning to the earlier biblical passage.

In the mid-1990s, a group of dispensationalist theologians tried to carve a middle path between dispensationalism and covenant theology—this became known as *progressive dispensationalism*. It allowed for an already/not yet approach to the kingdom of God and the covenants of promise. Rather than the *literal*-grammatical-historical method followed by classical and revised dispensationalists, this new group practiced a *literary*-grammatical-historical method. This slight hermeneutical shift allowed for more continuity between Israel and the church by rejecting the traditional (and controverted) two-peoples-of-God framework. Progressive dispensationalists viewed Israel and the church as two salvation-historical embodiments of the one people of God. Jewish Christians, then, are part of the church but still have claims on the promises God made to the nation of Israel.

Some contemporary covenant theologians have sought to distance themselves from the supersessionist implications of traditional covenant theology. Others argue for a future for Israel within the context of covenant theology (Rom. 11:25–26). The most popular landing spot, the *via media*, is *new covenant theology* or *progressive covenantalism*, a view that holds that God's revelation is revealed progressively over time and that this occurs through covenants that find their fulfillment in Christ. God's unified plan/promise climaxes in the new covenant. All of these theological systems are moving closer to each other on three important hermeneutical issues: Israel, the church, and the land.

Why does definitional clarity matter in this area? Well, what you decide in regard to dispensationalism will affect almost every area of your personal theology and the way you read your Bible. This does not mean, however, that those who follow one of the other theological systems are not one of the cool kids—we all are (John 17:21). The dispensational/covenantal divide has led to a lot of ingroup/outgroup categorizations. It would be preferable to practice hospitality and recognize there's a lot of room here for diverse interpretive practices as expressions of who we are in Christ.

2

THE DOCTRINE OF REVELATION

(Bibliology)

Revelation

The idea of revelation can seem rather mysterious, maybe even a bit spooky. For many, it conjures up ideas of deeply religious people having ecstatic experiences in which a divine being communicates to them. Christians may think of ancient prophets boldly issuing proclamations of "thus says the Lord" or even of the last book of the Bible, filled with all sorts of strange images. No wonder revelation can sound like an idea far removed from our day-to-day lives.

But revelation is a wonderful reality that makes our relationship with the living God possible. Think about it. We are tiny creatures in a vast universe; God is the unlimited, eternal Creator of all. Not only is He a being far greater than the universe He has made, but He is also separate from that universe (since He is Creator and it is created). On our own, we could never know Him or anything about Him. He must make Himself known.

THIS IS WHY GOD'S WORK OF REVELATION IS SUCH A GRACIOUS BLESSING. WITHOUT IT, WE COULD NEVER KNOW GOD.

This is exactly what revelation is about: God disclosing to human beings who He is, what He does, and what He wants for us. His self-disclosure not only reveals personal facts (factual knowledge), but it also makes it possible to have a relationship with Him (personal knowledge). This is why God's work of revelation is such a gracious blessing. Without it, we could never know God.

Who has received revelation from God? In one sense, everyone has. This is called *general revelation*, God's self-disclosure to all people everywhere. Scripture tells us God does this in various ways. He reveals Himself through creation itself (Ps. 19:1–6; Rom. 1:18–25), through His providential working in nature (Acts 14:14–18) and history (Acts 17:22–31), and even in the human conscience (Rom. 2:12–16). General revelation indirectly communicates general truths about God, such as His existence, glory, power, holiness, and goodness. But its message lacks specifics beyond those generalities. This limits its effect.

Some have argued that general revelation, despite its limited message, is still sufficient to potentially save anyone who responds positively to it. Scripture indicates that this is unlikely. For one thing, Paul insists that the message of general revelation is *not* sufficient. He argues that saving faith comes through the specific message of the gospel of Christ (Rom. 10:13–17). Further, even if general revelation were sufficient to save, no one left to their own devices responds rightly anyway. Instead, they suppress general revelation and turn their hearts to worship something other than God. Consequently, general revelation leads only to universal condemnation (Rom. 1:18–25).

If we are to be saved, we need revelation in another sense. This is called *special revelation*, which is God's direct self-disclosure to specific people at specific times with a specific message or appearance. The Scriptures give us many examples of special revelation in biblical history. These include *theophanies* or visible manifestations of God (e.g., Gen. 18:1–19; 32:24–32; Ex. 3:1–4; 13:21; 33:8–23), direct speech (Ex. 3:1–4:17; 19:3–7; 1 Sam. 3:1–11; Acts 26:12–16), dreams (Gen. 20; Dan. 2; Matt. 1:18–24), visions (Isa. 6:1–10; Dan. 10:4–20; Acts 10:9–17), angels (e.g., Dan. 9:20–22; Luke 1:26–38), prophets (e.g., 2 Sam. 12:1–15; Jer. 1:1–3; Isa. 38:1–8), and miraculous events (Deut. 4:32–35; John 20:30–31). But Scripture also affirms that there is one form of special revelation that surpasses all others: Jesus Christ, who is God in the flesh (John 1:1–18; 14:7–11; Heb. 1:1–3). The gospel message through which we are saved is all about Him—and for good reason, since we come to know God through Him.

There is another form of special revelation different from the others: Scripture. What makes Scripture unique is that it preserves special revelation for God's people. All other forms of special revelation, including Jesus Christ in His first coming, happened in the past. Scripture preserves those past events of special revelation so that we have access to them today. What's more, the words of Scripture themselves are special revelation, for Scripture itself is the very Word of God. This important reality is explained in greater detail in the next term.

6 Inspiration

In English, we use the word "inspire" in various ways. A leader may "inspire" his followers to greater devotion; a poet may be "inspired" by someone she loves; an artist may be "inspired" to paint by a beautiful landscape; an athlete may be "inspired" to greater achievements by a competitor.

But the doctrine of inspiration is far removed from these ideas. This theological term reflects the way 2 Timothy 3:16 is often translated in English: "All Scripture is inspired by God" (NASB). The word translated "inspired" is the Greek word *theopneustos*, which literally means "God-breathed." Paul is not merely affirming that Scripture is inspiring to us (though to be sure it is); he is affirming that it comes from God. God breathes out or speaks all Scripture, thereby making it His very Word. Peter makes a similar point in 2 Peter 1:20–21: the biblical writers "spoke from God as they were carried along by the Holy Spirit" (ESV).

What does the Bible teach about its own inspiration? First of all, as we saw in the passages above, inspiration means that the Bible is God's Word through the work of the Holy Spirit. What's more, 2 Timothy 3:16 insists this is true of *all* Scripture. Many people like certain parts of the Bible, but they want to ignore or reject other parts they do not like. The Bible's teaching about itself simply will not allow us to pick and choose the parts we want, like some kind of buffet. All of it is God's Word.

This extends even to the specific words of Scripture. Some have argued that the Holy Spirit only gave the biblical writers revelatory ideas in their heads—and then left them alone to put those ideas into their own words as best they could, warts and all. This would mean that the words of Scripture are merely the words of men. But Scripture equates its words with God's words (cf. Matt. 19:4–5 with Gen. 2:24; cf. Rom. 9:17 with Ex. 9:16), which is why Jesus (Matt. 22:32, 44–45; John 10:35) and Paul (Gal. 3:16) both appeal to specific words in Old Testament Scripture to prove a point from God's Word.

But here's the interesting thing. While the Bible insists that it is God's Word down to its very syllables, it also insists it was written by human authors. And these human writers were not merely taking dictation from God. They genuinely authored the words they wrote (e.g., Deut. 1:1; Luke 1:1–4; Acts 1:1; John 21:24–25; the opening of most New Testament epistles), making their different personalities and writing styles so evident in Scripture. Yet the Holy Spirit oversaw the whole process to ensure that the words written were exactly what God wanted written. Scripture thus has a genuine dual authorship (e.g., Mark 7:9–13; Acts 4:25)—what theologians call *concursus*. Think how this affects the way you read your Bible. You can read, study, and understand the Bible the way you would other human books, but in doing so, you are hearing directly from God Himself (1 Cor. 10:11).

By communicating to us in the written words of human authors, God preserves His revelation and makes it widely accessible. Written revelation can be preserved because it can be copied. Technically speaking, only the original manuscripts of Scripture were fully inspired, since the Holy Spirit superintended the work as the human authors wrote. Those original manuscripts—written in Hebrew (or Aramaic in a few places) in the Old Testament and Greek in the New Testament—no longer exist, but for centuries they were copied carefully by hand. We still have many of these ancient copies through which the original text is preserved. By studying and comparing them, the discipline of *textual criticism* makes the original text available to us. Written revelation can also be widely disseminated because it can be translated accurately into any language. We know this because New Testament writers sometimes quote from the Greek translation of the Hebrew Old Testament (called the *Septuagint* or LXX). A good translation, then, accurately reflects the original text. God's inspired, written Word is still available to us today, even if we don't speak Greek or Hebrew.

Let's summarize what we've said into a definition of what is called *verbal-plenary inspiration*. In His work of inspiration, the Holy Spirit superintended the human authors as they wrote Scripture so that all Scripture, even down to the very words in the original writings, is God's Word as well as the words of the human writers. This has huge implications for what Scripture is, as we see in the next term.

7 The Characteristics of Scripture

This term is actually more of a category by which we can group together several terms about the nature of Scripture. Scripture's characteristics are rooted in its origin as the inspired, written Word of God. What are they?

Let's first consider Scripture's *authority*. Since Scripture is inspired, it is God's Word, and so it carries His authority. What kind of authority does God have? He is the sovereign King of the universe, with the authority to command and the right to be obeyed. In addition, because He knows everything and is completely truthful, He has the authority of the ultimate expert on everything and the right to be believed. He's also completely holy and pure; thus He has the moral authority to always be trusted. Since Scripture carries God's authority, we must similarly obey, believe, and trust God's Word.

God is the highest authority in the universe; consequently, there is no higher authority than Scripture. Protestant theologians call this the doctrine of *sola scriptura*, Latin for "Scripture alone." It means that the Bible is our only final authority (similar to the way the US Constitution is the final law of the land). No human authority can legitimately equal or supersede Scripture.

It's clear that Jesus and the apostles considered Scripture God's authoritative Word, both in what they said about Scripture's authority (e.g., Matt. 5:17–18; John 10:35) and how they argued from it (e.g., Matt. 4:1–11; 22:23–33). Unfortunately, too many Christians today are tempted to disbelieve, disobey, or distrust Scripture. The world encourages us to listen to other authorities and to limit or even dismiss Scripture's authority, and our own hearts are prone to rebel. But failing to submit to Scripture's authority is a failure to submit to God, a fool's errand indeed.

Another characteristic of Scripture, closely related to its authority, is Scripture's *inerrancy*. This doctrine maintains that Scripture never affirms error but always affirms what is true. Inerrancy is supported by biblical teaching (e.g., Ps. 119; Prov. 30:5; John 10:34–35; 17:17) and by the character of God Himself, for God knows everything and is never mistaken in His knowledge (1 John 3:10; Ps. 139; Heb. 4:13), and He cannot lie (Heb. 6:18; Titus 1:2). If Scripture, which is His very Word, affirmed error, then God would either be lying or mistaken in His knowledge, neither of which is possible.

When pondering inerrancy, keep a few things in mind. First, inerrancy applies to the original writings, not manuscript copies or translations. If a copyist accidentally wrote down a wrong word, or if a translator translates incorrectly, this does not affect the inerrancy of the original writings. Second, inerrancy applies to the meaning of the biblical text; it does not guarantee that my interpretation is correct. If someone thinks my interpretation of a text is incorrect, she is not denying inerrancy. Third, inerrancy does not demand hyper-literalism or precisionism; it takes the genre and ordinary language of Scripture into account. For example, inerrancy would not demand that Jesus is a plant because He said He is the vine (John 15:1), nor would it insist that all quotations in Scripture are verbatim rather than paraphrases. Finally, inerrancy does not mean there are not some difficult texts in Scripture that critics charge as errors and use to deny inerrancy. But a great many of these "problem passages" already have adequate solutions consistent with inerrancy. And if there are a few problem passages to which we still do not have a convincing solution (given our limited knowledge of the ancient world or some other limitation in our current knowledge), Scripture's teaching about itself and its track record give us confidence that an adequate solution will present itself once more relevant information becomes available.

This last point about inerrancy recalls a closely related term: Scripture's *infallibility*. Traditionally, evangelicals have used this term synonymously with inerrancy, and some still do today. In this sense, Scripture's infallibility means that it is not liable to error or failure. More recently, however, some theologians use the term to deny Scripture's inerrancy. They might say, for example, that Scripture is "infallible" in the sense that it always affirms what is true theologically or practically, but that it makes mistakes when it comes other matters, such as historical fact. In the end, when used in a way consistent with inerrancy, infallibility is a perfectly good term to use, but when someone uses it, be sure to ask what they mean.

Another important characteristic of Scripture is its *sufficiency*. This means that God communicates to us in Scripture all that we need to know today to be saved, to live in a way that pleases Him, and to evaluate all other claims of authority (2 Tim. 3:15–17; James 1:18; 1 Peter 1:22–23; Ps. 19:7–14; 119; Prov. 30:5–6). This does not mean that God gives us everything we need to know about anything; Scripture is not an encyclopedia of all knowledge. But when it comes to our relationship with the living God and our worldview, it is all we need and absolutely indispensable. Unfortunately, sometimes we can be tempted to doubt Scripture's sufficiency even in those areas to which it speaks. In those times we may ignore it, or "correct" it in our minds, or assume it has nothing to say about our need, or want to supplement it with human wisdom and experience to "improve" it. All such attitudes betray a denial of Scripture's sufficiency.

Scripture's authority, inerrancy, and sufficiency are well and good, but what if you can't understand it? This is where Scripture's *clarity* (or *perspicuity*—a term not particularly perspicuous!) comes in. This doctrine maintains that the meaning of the biblical text is available to human beings who want to understand it (Deut. 6:4–7; Ps. 19:7–8; 119:130; John 5:39; 2 Tim. 3:15–4:2). After all, it is God's Word, and He is willing and able to communicate to us. To claim that Scripture is impossible to understand is to imply that God is not a competent communicator or that He really does not want to reveal Himself at all.

The doctrine of Scripture's clarity does not mean that every passage is easy to understand; some texts are quite difficult (2 Peter 3:15–16). But even in those cases, their meaning is still available. And in any case, the basic message of Scripture (with the gospel at its core) is clearly taught throughout Scripture (John 5:39). No one who has read or heard Scripture, and who has the normal capacity to understand human communication, can legitimately claim that its basic message was inaccessible to them.

Scripture's authority, inerrancy, and sufficiency mean it *ought* to be disseminated as widely as possible; its clarity means it *can* be widely disseminated. These characteristics make Scripture unique among all other writings. But this raises another important question: what writings deserve to be included in the category of Scripture? The next term addresses this question.

The Canon of Scripture

Quite obviously, the biblical canon has nothing to do with an artillery piece (i.e., a cannon); it refers to a body of literature—specifically, the collection of books comprising the Bible. These books were written by various human authors over a period of about 1,500 years. Over time those writings were recognized as God's Word and collected by God's people. Other Jewish and Christian religious writings were also written over that span of time, of course, but these were not deemed to be Scripture.

This is where the term "canon" comes in. It derives from the Hebrew word *qaneh* and the Greek word *kanōn*, both referring to a measuring rod. We might say, then, that these books alone "measure up" to what it takes to be included in Scripture, thereby making them the standard by which we should "measure" our lives. And this is true because these particular writings alone are inspired by God (in the sense described above). The biblical canon, then, is the collection of all writings that are divinely inspired. For Protestant Christians, the canon consists solely of the 39 books of the Old Testament and the 27 books of the New.

The biblical canon raises several important questions. First, who determined whether a particular writing was canonical? Clearly, God's people have played an important role in this process, since they are the ones who collected, preserved, and used these writings as Scripture. But some traditions (e.g., Roman Catholicism) have stressed the role that the church has played in the collection of the canonical books. They think of the canon as *an authoritative list of books*, for the collection was authorized by the church. But since the books were inspired by God, they are inherently authoritative—regardless of whether the church authorized them or not. It is better, then, to think of the canon as a list of *authoritative books*. God chose which books He would inspire and thereby authorize. Over time God's people (through the leading of the Holy Spirit) simply *recognized* the inspiration of those canonical books and collected them.

But that raises another question. How did God's people recognize which books were inspired Scripture? What factors did they take into consideration? Several could be mentioned. First, in regard to human authorship, the book was written by a prophet or an apostle (or a close associate). After all, these men were accredited spokesmen for God (Deut. 13:1–3; 18:18–22; 1 Cor. 14:37–38). Second, the book does not affirm error, because any book that is God's Word cannot err (cf. Deut. 18:22; Prov. 30:5–6). Third, the book must be consistent with truth that God has already revealed, since God does not contradict Himself (Deut. 13:1–5; Gal. 1:8–9; cf. Acts 17:11). Fourth, in many cases a book's status as Scripture is affirmed by other prophets and apostles and by Jesus Himself. For example, Jesus and the apostles treated the Hebrew canon of their day (the 39 books of our Old Testament) as Scripture, God's authoritative Word. In addition, Peter refers to Paul's writings as Scripture (2 Peter 3:16), and in 1 Timothy 5:18 Paul quotes from Luke 10:7 as Scripture.

Fifth, the book has come to be widely accepted as inspired Scripture by God's people. God has declared that His Word will endure (Ps. 119:89, 160; Isa. 40:8; Matt. 5:18; 24:35), and since He is sovereign over everything, it makes sense that He would providentially work in history to preserve His inspired Word. He did this *for* His people so that later generations of believers could have access to the Word of God long after it was first written down (Deut. 31:9–13; 1 Cor. 10:11; Matt. 22:31). But He also preserves Scripture *through* His people. Because the Spirit is at work actively in the hearts of believers to receive and understand His inspired Word (1 Cor. 2:11–16), that Word will work powerfully in their lives whenever they read and hear it (Heb. 4:12; 2 Tim. 3:15–17). That being the case, God's people will recognize an inspired writing for what it is. The providential preservation of God's Word—and the powerful working of the Holy Spirit with His Word—mean that in time God's people will come to universally recognize those writings He inspired. The 66 books of our Old Testament and New Testament today are the only books to receive universal acceptance among all orthodox Christians.

The canon of Scripture raises one final question. Is the canon closed, or are there other writings not yet recognized that He has or will inspire? Any budding archaeologist hoping to find a missing biblical book should expect to be disappointed. The canon is closed; we already have all the books God inspired. This may be implied in Revelation 22:18–19, where John warns about adding to the book of Revelation. But this warning could have implications for the closing of the canon as a whole. After all, Revelation is the last book in the Bible, it tells us how the whole story ends, and it was the last canonical book to be written. It is a fitting closing to our Bible, suggesting that the canon is closed.

But there is a more important reason why the canon is closed. Jesus is the ultimate revelation of God (Heb. 1:1–3), the one to whom the whole Old Testament testifies (John 5:39). Jesus promised the apostles that the Spirit would help them to remember and preserve His words and works (John 14:25–26). They are chosen by Christ as His Spirit-empowered eyewitnesses, authorized to found His church (Eph. 2:20). The New Testament writings, written by the apostles and their close associates, preserve and interpret the ultimate revelation of God in Christ. What more do we need?

3

THE DOCTRINE OF GOD

(Theology Proper)

The Trinity

Several years ago in a theology class, I remember seeing a comic strip with three Gandalf-looking characters regally standing guard over a box. The pencil-drawn figures looked intently at the table in front of them. The caption read, "After months of intensive effort, Prof. Mortzman and his fellow theologians finally succeed in putting God in a box." This humorous statement is a great reminder for us in regard to the limitations present in the language we use to "describe" God (Ps. 145:3; Isa. 55:8–9). It is also an important reminder that getting our theology right helps to order our worship and understanding of the gospel (Isa. 43:10–11). So, while there will be mystery associated with the study of God, it is not an impenetrable venture (Rom. 11:33).

"The Trinity" is the theological term used to describe the doctrine that there is one God who exists eternally as three divine, coequal, and distinct persons: the Father, the Son, and the Holy Spirit, who all possess the same attributes or perfections and work together in the world in an economy of love. The word "Trinity" (Gk. *trias*; Lat. *trinitas*) is not a biblical term, so you won't find it by searching a concordance. But it is an inference drawn from the text. It rightly encompasses the Bible's teaching on (a) monotheism, the belief in one God (Deut. 6:4; Rom. 3:30); (b) the equal divinity of the Father, Son, and Holy Spirit (1 Cor. 8:6; Eph. 4:6; John 5:18; 1 John 5:20; Acts 5:3–4; 1 Cor. 6:19); and (c) the distinct divine persons of the Father, Son, and Holy Spirit (John 5:31–36; 8:16–18; 14:26; 15:26). The Trinitarian formula is that there is one God, God is three persons, and each person is fully God. This is the way to faithfully render Scripture's teachings; indeed, views that divert from one of these planks have been considered unorthodox (see **Trinitarian Heresies**) and are not valid options for those seeking to live under the authority of God's Word in line with the church's historic teaching.

This conceptualization of the Bible's judgments about divine tri-unity was partially formalized in AD 325 at the First Council of Nicaea, and later clarified in AD 381 at the First Council of Constantinople and in AD 451 at the Council of Chalcedon. These later councils captured the Bible's Trinitarian teaching. For example, the baptismal formula in Matthew 28:19 directs the earliest Christ followers to baptize converts "in the name of the Father and of the Son and of the Holy Spirit." Paul's benediction in 2 Corinthians 13:14 reveals a Trinitarian awareness: "The grace of the Lord Jesus Christ, and the love of God, and the fellowship of the Holy Spirit be with you all." Later in Ephesians 2:17–18, he describes the preaching ministry of Jesus, and then explains, "For through him [Jesus] we both have access in one Spirit to the Father" (ESV). The later councils referenced these and other larger blocks of Scripture as evidence that Trinitarian theology is a proper doctrinal judgment (e.g., Gal. 4:4–6; 2 Thess. 2:13–15; John 14:16; 15:26; 16:13–15).

Often in reading theology readers come across the *economic Trinity* and the *immanent Trinity*—what's the difference? Well, we are not saying there are two different Trinities; rather, these are two models for understanding the Trinity. The economic Trinity describes the distinct roles, operations, and workings of the Trinity—what the three persons do in creating, sustaining, and redeeming the world. This is useful so long as we recognize the undivided work of the Trinity through the doctrine of *appropriations*, in which one member of the Godhead may be emphasized in context but all are involved in the action (e.g., predestination, Eph. 1:4–6; 1 Peter 1:1–2; John 6:70; 13:18a; 1 Cor. 2:10–11). It is still appropriate to speak of the unique redemptive work of Jesus on the cross, or the Holy Spirit's activity in the application of that work. This is Trinitarian love: the Father sent the Son as an atoning sacrifice, and the Spirit comes to apply that sacrifice to the objects of God's love.

God's eternal identity, meanwhile, is highlighted through the use of the so-called immanent or ontological Trinity. It describes distinctions in the eternal relations within the Godhead, such as paternity (John 5:26), sonship or generation

(John 3:16), and procession or spiration (John 14:26; 15:26). Some find the economic-immanent distinction helpful, while others think it creates more confusion since it doesn't map sufficiently onto the way Scripture speaks of God's divine life and administration of the world (John 1:1–18; 8:42). A word to the wise—beware of over-abstraction in Trinitarian theology!

Clear thinking about the Trinity also helps our prayer life. Often we generically address our prayers to God, but we can be more precise (see **Worship**). The biblical model is praying to the Father, in the name of the Son, by the power of the Holy Spirit (John 16:23; Eph. 3:16; 5:20; Col. 3:17; Rom. 8:26). This allows us to be more fully aware of what's going on when we pray. Following the model of the Lord's Prayer can assist us in rightly ordering our prayer life away from our tendency toward our self-centeredness and toward Him who is faithful to hear and answer (Matt. 6:9–13; John 14:13–14; 16:3). One practical step could be to end your prayers in the name of the Father, Son, and Holy Spirit. This has been a practice of Christians throughout history, and it can remind us of the centrality of Trinitarian theology to all of life.

10 Trinitarian Heresies

Sometimes in class I will jokingly say, "Heretics are God's gift to the church . . ." I wait to let that settle in for a moment and then conclude, ". . . because they allow us to clarify the truth." In relation to the Trinity, heretics have usually failed to maintain—or have overemphasized—one of these three vital planks: (a) God's oneness and threeness, (b) the deity of Christ or the Holy Spirit, and (c) the distinctions and equality between the three persons.

The view that Jesus was a mere man until His baptism, when the Spirit fell on Him and He received God's power in a unique way, has come to be called *dynamic monarchianism*, or *adoptionism*. This second-century view wanted to protect monotheism, but did so at the expense of Jesus' deity. The First Council of Nicaea in 325 rejected this adoptionist view: "We believe in one Lord, Jesus Christ, the only Son of God, eternally begotten of the Father." Adoptionist views are still present among theologians today, and they create problems doctrinally since they (a) destabilize the notion of Jesus' sacrifice as the God-man, and (b) raise the specter of merit as a means for acceptance before God.

Others, wanting to maintain monotheism and the divinity of Father, Son, and Holy Spirit, thought the best way to describe the Trinity was with names representing modes of being. This view came to be known as *modalistic monarchianism*, or *Sabellianism*. A third-century theologian, Sabellius taught that God revealed Himself as the Father in the Old Testament, then as the Son during the life of Jesus, and finally as the Holy Spirit during the age of the church. One God, three subsequent modes. A difficulty with this view, though, is that it doesn't deal satisfactorily with the texts where all three members of the Godhead are simultaneously active or speaking, such as at Jesus' baptism (Matt. 3:16–17), His transfiguration (Matt. 17:5), and even in His prayers (John 14:16; Luke 23:46). Another significant problem, known as *patripassianism*, is the belief that the Father suffered or died on the cross in the appearance of Jesus. This was deemed unacceptable and so the church responded with the doctrine of the impassibility of God. The Father could not die; only Jesus, the God-man, by adding human nature, could suffer and die.

Tritheism is the view that the Father, Son, and Holy Spirit are three distinct deities. This is a form of polytheism and is the opposite of modalism. This view has never been seriously considered historically, though there may be a sense that some forms of contemporary social trinitarianism come close to this view. It's likely that some church attenders hold a soft form of this view, especially if they view the members of the Trinity sitting in heaven and holding court in a manner similar to Zeus, Hades, and Poseidon among the Greek pantheon, seen for example in the *Percy Jackson and the Olympians* novels or films.

Macedonianism is the view that the Holy Spirit is not fully divine; it gets its name from Macedonius of Constantinople, who is thought to have held it. This fourth-century heresy is also known as *pneumatomachianism*, which means "spirit fighters," for these heretics were resisting the church's teaching that the Holy Spirit is fully God. Some sought to understand the Spirit as a liminal figure—neither God nor a creature. A close contemporary analogy would be "the Force" in *Star Wars*. This heresy was condemned at the First Council of Constantinople in AD 381. This is why, rather than saying "may the Force be with you" in our benedictions, we declare, "May the . . . Holy Spirit be with you" (2 Cor. 13:14).

Unitarianism rejects God's tri-personality in its emphasis on God's unity. It emerged from Arian teachings, which denied Christ's deity, and thus was rejected as heterodox. The contemporary expression of this view is traced to Faustus Socinus (1539–1604) as he revived the idea that only God the Father is truly divine and that Jesus, while deserving honor, is not. God's tri-personality and singular essence is not rational. Thus Jesus, while being a good example, does not share in the identity of the God of Israel. This perspective became central to the Enlightenment's perspective on God, with its emphasis on rationality. The major warning for us from Socinus's example is to never assume the Trinity is simply irrelevant, illogical, or irrational. In addition, understanding the Trinity is important for thinking accurately about the atoning work of Christ on the cross—Jesus' death on the cross is not just an example to follow—it is much more (see **Atonement**).

11 God's Attributes

In the 1987 classic movie *The Princess Bride*, there's an exchange between Vizzini, the film's antagonist, and his henchman Inigo Montoya, in which Vizzini states, "He didn't fall?!

Inconceivable!" to which Montoya responds, "You keep using that word. I do not think it means what you think it means." Our goal is to not be like Vizzini. We want to be clear on several key terms related to Scripture's teaching on God's attributes, so that we worship Him as He wants to be known—not as we make Him out to be in our own minds and thoughts.

HIS NATURE IS ONE ESSENCE IN PERFECT SIMPLICITY.

The attributes of God are those characteristics or qualities of His Trinitarian nature that are critical to a virtuous understanding of His essence. These spiritual perfections are shared by all three members of the Godhead and reveal what constitutes Deity (Col. 2:9; *theotetos*). These are not aggregate parts of God, since He is not a compound being. He exists in simplicity as an indivisible being. His attributes are therefore not portions in His nature—they describe Him as He is. Remembering this will help us not to elevate one attribute above another, which would contradict God's *simplicity* (e.g., His love over His righteousness). It would also contradict God's *unity*, which brings to the fore the idea that His nature is one essence in perfect simplicity. There is only one essential truth in the universe, and He is both an absolute and personal God (Isa. 44:6–8).

The unity and simplicity of God suggests an indivisible being, which brings to the fore God's *immutability*. He is unchanging and unchangeable in His nature (Ps. 102:25–27;

Mal. 3:6; James 1:17) and in His plan (Ezek. 24:14; Phil. 1:6). God is constant—but what about those passages that suggest God changes His mind (Ex. 32:14; Isa. 38:1–8; Jonah 3:4–10)? There are likely figures of speech involved in these narratives. In addition, the stories are framed in a contingent way—a condition is present that, if met, would change the originally stated prediction. Thankfully, God can always be trusted in regard to what He has said He will do.

These three attributes—simplicity, unity, and immutability—are part of the traditional listing of divine attributes not shared with humanity. Another is *aseity*, which means that God is self-existent, uncaused, and the only necessary being. We get a glimpse into this in Exodus 3:14: "God said to Moses, 'I AM WHO I AM.'" It is in His nature to exist, as the "to be" verb suggests. God's aseity or independence gives us confidence that He is the ultimate source of everything (Rev. 4:11)—and as the only self-existent being in the universe, all other claimants are not worthy of our ultimate affection or devotion (John 5:26; Ps. 94:8–11). This theological term supports a load-bearing idea, the Creator-creature distinction. Indeed, most aberrant views of God merge these two ideas at some point.

God is also *infinite*, which means He has no limitations. He has no beginning or end. Time or linear sequencing of activities do not bind Him (Ps. 90:2). In regard to space, He is present everywhere at the same time. This is also described as *omnipresence*, the infinity of God in relation to space

(Ps. 139:7–12). In relation to knowledge, God's infinity is described as His *omniscience*: He has perfect and infinite knowledge of everything, including actual and potential events (Ps. 147:4–5; Matt. 11:21). In relation to power, God's infinity is described as His *omnipotence*: "He does whatever He pleases" (Ps. 115:3 NASB; see Isa. 40:10–31). He is able to do whatever He wills. This power operates within the limits of, or in harmony with, His nature (Matt. 3:9; 26:53). The assurance for us here is that nothing is too hard for the Lord to accomplish if He wills it. These "omni" statements also remind us that God is without material substance and free from all temporal limitations. A body localizes, but as spirit God is everywhere (John 4:24).

Other divine attributes revealed in Scripture are parallel to human experience in some way. God's *wisdom* indicates He uses the best possible means to accomplish His eternal purposes (Ps. 104:24). This attribute functions in conjunction with His omniscience; it is through His wisdom that He judges righteously and applies His infinite knowledge to bring ultimate glory to Himself (Rom. 2:2; 1 Tim. 1:17). God is also *holy—transcendent*, set apart, and morally pure in His nature (Ex. 15:11; Isa. 6:1–5; 1 John 1:5; Rev. 4:8). He is the highest good, exalted above His creation.

Though utterly transcendent, God participates in the lives of creatures who are marred by sin and injustice (Hab. 1:2, 5, 12). This reminds us that God is also *immanent*; He relates to and is involved in creaturely existence. Isaiah 57:15 keeps God's transcendence and immanence in balance: "For this is what the high and exalted One says . . . I live in a high and holy place, but also with the one who is contrite and lowly in spirit" (NASB). Many aberrant views of God today overemphasize either God's transcendence or God's immanence. Our goal should be to keep both truths in balance.

God's *love* is an attribute where He delights in His own perfections, in humanity as a reflection of His image, and in all He has created (Isa. 63:9; John 3:16; Acts 14:17; 1 John 4:8, 16). It first indicates an intra-Trinitarian love the persons of the Trinity have for one another (John 3:35; 14:31), sometimes expressed by the Spirit's activity in the world (John 15:26; 16:14; Gal. 4:6). God's love does not negate His holiness; as with His other attributes, these two function in harmony within His being (Deut. 32:4; 1 Tim. 1:5). Further, God's attribute of goodness, which reflects His loving concern for His creation, cannot be ignored (Acts 14:15–17). His *goodness* is directed toward our conformity to the image of His Son, such that anything in our lives may be understood as for our good (Rom. 8:28–29).

> **PRAYING AND MEDITATING ON GOD'S ATTRIBUTES HELPS US TO KNOW GOD AS HE'S REVEALED HIMSELF, RATHER THAN AS WE DEFINE HIM IN THE MIDST OF OUR TROUBLES.**

"Praying" God's attributes is a way for us to keep our perspective during times of suffering and anguish. We can gather the

Scriptures that refer to God's *justice*, His righteous dealings with His creation, read and meditate on them, and then allow them to inform our prayers. For example, if you are overwhelmed by an unjust situation, reading Isaiah 30:18 or 61:8 can renew your perspective. If you wonder why the circumstance has occurred, meditate on Job 34:12: "It is unthinkable that God would do wrong, that the Almighty would pervert justice." Praying and meditating on God's attributes helps us to know God as He's revealed Himself, rather than as we define Him in the midst of our troubles.

12 — God's Sovereignty and Human Responsibility

One divine attribute deserves special consideration, since it is the focal point for much theological debate and confusion. The sovereignty or *freedom of God* is the idea that by His power, God has planned and now guides the events of the universe along with the actions of His creatures. The first part of this definition is evident in Ephesians 1:11, where Paul claims that God "works all things according to the counsel of his will" (ESV). God has a plan, and remembering this can give us confidence and hope amid pain and suffering. He is the master and sole ruler of the universe. He rules by His *decree*, which is His eternal, purposeful plan by which He determined everything that would occur. It is through this that

God guides the events of the world. This part of the definition emerges in Isaiah 46:10, where God is seen as the one "declaring the end from the beginning . . . saying, 'My counsel shall stand, and I will accomplish all my purpose'" (ESV).

The sovereignty or freedom of God is supported by two broader teachings in Scripture: creation and providence. Genesis 1:1 begins, "In the beginning God created . . ." These words anchor an idea central throughout Scripture: God is the *creator* of all things, and because of this we can have confidence that He also sustains His creation. This latter aspect of the doctrine is known as the *providence* of God— His continuing work that sustains and preserves the world He created, and that assures that the universe arrives at its God-glorifying intended end. His original act of creating the universe out of nothing is known as *creatio ex nihilo* (Lat. "creation out of nothing"). This means He did not use existing materials in His act of creation; rather, He spoke all things into existence (Rom. 4:17), a belief that ultimately comes "by faith" (Heb. 11:3).

Maintaining God as the Creator of all things (Rev. 4:11) has been especially important since the mid-nineteenth century, when evolution emerged as a competing theory for the origins of the universe. Theologians have offered various responses to it, from wholesale rejection to full integration. The focus for the debate often hinges on the age of the earth. Those rejecting evolution, often referred to as *young-earth creationists*, think the universe was created as recently as six thousand years ago and seek to read Genesis 1–2 literally. *Old-earth creationists*, on the other hand, contend that the universe is significantly older. Some of them seek to fully integrate evolution with Christianity (*theistic evolutionists*), while others do not (*progressive creationists*). But all old-earth advocates read portions of Genesis 1 non-literally and incorporate scientific findings in ways young-earth creationists do not. Much of the debate revolves around how to understand "day" (Heb. *yom*) in Genesis 1: is it a literal twenty-four-hour day, or a longer period of time? While difficult to determine exegetically, one key point is that Exodus 20:8–11 grounds the fourth commandment on a literal reading of the days of Genesis 1. Whichever view is accepted, though, the historicity of Genesis 1–2 and the literal-historical-grammatical approach to interpretation should be maintained. God's original work of creation and continuing work of providence provide a foundation for understanding His sovereignty and human responsibility.

It is important to distinguish the decree of God from life's imperfections. God is able to work through these and other actions of His creatures in order to accomplish His will. Paul reminds us of this in Romans 8:28: "And we know that for those who love God all things work together for good, for those who are called according to his purpose" (ESV). The fall of humanity in the garden of Eden did not result in the loss of God's plan, nor remove His control over the world. The good news is that when life seems out of control, we can rest assured that *God* is still in control. He cares about seemingly insignificant details in our lives (Matt. 10:29–31); Christ continues to uphold all of creation (Col. 1:16–17; Heb. 1:3); and God's purpose in the world cannot finally be thwarted (Job 42:2; Lam. 3:37–39). God's sovereignty is a biblical teaching that should be a source of immense comfort in this life. So, while we may be tempted to question *why* He has allowed certain events to occur, biblical wisdom calls us away from such questions (Isa. 45:7–9; Rom. 9:19–21).

If God is sovereign to this degree, is there a place for human responsibility in the affairs of the world? These two ideas, God's sovereignty and human responsibility, seem to stand in a paradoxical relationship; Scripture, though, places them in a compatible relationship. This view is known as *compatibilism*. It contends that divine sovereignty and human responsibility cohere. God is sovereign, but not in such a way that human responsibility is destroyed. Humans are morally responsible for their actions, but never to the degree that God's sovereignty is redefined or diminished to being contingent on human actions.

This compatibilist framework is apparent in Scripture. Divine sovereignty is evident in Luke 22:21–22a: "But the hand of [Judas], who is going to betray me, is with mine on the table. The Son of Man will go as it has been decreed." Judas's betrayal was predetermined to occur. And yet human responsibility is also evident in Luke 22:22b: "But woe to that man who betrays him!" A similar compatibilistic understanding of

Christ's crucifixion is evident in Acts 2:23, where God's plan and human agency are both highlighted. Divine sovereignty and human responsibility are also evident in regard to salvation. Divine sovereignty, or in this case election, is marked at the beginning of 2 Thessalonians 2:13: "But we ought always to thank God for you, brothers and sisters loved by the Lord, because God chose you as firstfruits to be saved through the sanctifying work of the Spirit." Then human response appears at the end of the verse: "through belief in the truth." (See **Election**.)

Scripture never separates divine sovereignty and human responsibility. Those who disagree with this claim may be described as *incompatibilists*, since for them these two teachings cannot be reconciled. Scriptures such as Luke 13:34 represent real human choices and reveal self-imposed limitations on God's sovereignty. An incompatibilist believes the causal nature of compatibilism is incompatible with *libertarian free will*, a view that human behavior is self-caused. The absolute sovereignty needed for the compatibilist position reduces free will to nothing, since free will must have the opportunity to do otherwise—or the concept is meaningless.

Another approach that maintains a high view of God's sovereignty, but with a libertarian view of free will, is *Molinism*, named after the sixteenth-century priest Luis de Molina. The way the interpretive dissonance between divine sovereignty and human responsibility is resolved is through the concept of *middle knowledge*, a type of knowledge that relies on "counterfactuals" of libertarian free choices. This seemingly allows for a resolution to the dilemma, since God is aware of all events that would arise based on all possible combinations of circumstances. God is therefore able to create a world with the outcomes He ordains while still granting libertarian free will to each person.

The doctrine of God's sovereignty matters first because it reminds us of His glory and that He alone is worthy of our worship. It also gives us comfort and security in the midst of disappointment and pain, for we know that our good and sovereign God governs the world through His decree. While this might leave some wishing for a different type of understanding of reality and free will, it is at least worth pondering: would we really want to live in a world in which God doesn't ordain what comes to pass?

4

THE DOCTRINE OF CHRIST

(Christology)

 The Incarnation of Christ

We all love Christmas. And why not? It's a festive time to give and receive gifts, take off work or school, have parties, eat good food, and spend time with family and friends. Many people acknowledge, of course, that Christmas is also a celebration of the birth of Jesus Christ. As Christians, we recognize that this birth is unlike that of any other great person. Indeed, Christmas commemorates an event of staggering proportions: the incarnation of the Son of God.

What are we celebrating at Christmas? What happened at the incarnation of the Son of God? The eternal second person of the Trinity (God the Son), without ceasing to be God in any way, took into union with Himself a human nature so that He became forever thereafter the God-man, Jesus Christ (John 1:14; Phil. 2:5–11). We will say more about the incarnated person of Christ in a later entry (see **The Hypostatic Union**), but here we must consider three important elements of this doctrine.

First, the incarnation presupposes that the Son of God existed long before His incarnation. This is called *Christ's preexistence*. In fact, because the Son is divine and therefore eternal, His is an *eternal* preexistence (John 1:1; 8:58; Heb. 1:8; Col. 1:16–17; Isa. 9:6; Rev. 1:17; 22:13). And the *preincarnate* Christ was not idle prior to His incarnation. Although His dwelling was in heaven (John 3:13, 16–17, 31) where He received all the glory He deserves (John 17:5), He was also active in the world in the Old Testament era. For example, He was the one by whom all things were created and sustained in existence (John 1:3; Col. 1:16–17). In addition, since the Son is the one who makes God known (John 1:18), it is possible that temporary visible manifestations of God in the Old Testament (theophanies) were, more specifically, visible manifestations of the second person of the Trinity (*Christophanies*).

Another important element of the incarnation was its accomplishment through the *virgin birth of Christ*. This means Jesus had no physical human father but was conceived by the miraculous power of the Holy Spirit in the womb of the virgin Mary, who remained a virgin until she gave birth to Jesus (Isa. 7:14; Matt. 1:18, 22–25; Luke 1:26–38). This doctrine does not undermine Jesus' full humanity, since Adam and Eve were also not conceived through sexual relations and yet were fully human and the parents of the whole human race.

Nor does this mean humans inherit their sinful natures from their physical fathers, for women (including Mary) as well as men are sinful by nature (Eph. 2:1–4). Mary thus could have passed sin on to Jesus even without any human male involved. Instead, it was the power of the Spirit who kept Jesus from inheriting a sinful nature (as Luke 1:35 suggests). What the virgin birth does stress is the uniqueness of Christ as the God-man and messianic deliverer of human beings in fulfillment of Scripture (see Isa. 7:14). And it is a powerful reminder that God is the one who must save us. "Salvation belongs to the LORD" (Jonah 2:9 ESV).

Finally, the incarnation undermines neither Christ's full deity nor His full humanity. As we saw earlier, His virgin birth does not make Him less than human; and as we will see in a later entry (**The Sinlessness of Christ**), neither does His sinlessness. Moreover, unlike Old Testament theophanies, which were only temporary visible manifestations of God, the incarnation is permanent. Christ took on a full human nature forever, so that He can be our eternal priest, king, and savior (Heb. 7:17; Dan. 7:14).

Yet His full, permanent humanity does not in any way undermine His full deity. Some have argued that in taking on full humanity Christ had to give up some of His divine attributes (e.g., omniscience and omnipotence). But since God's attributes are essential to who God is, Jesus could not give up any of those attributes without ceasing to be God (see **The Hypostatic Union**). Thus the claim that Jesus gave up His divine attributes is a mistaken attempt to understand the *kenosis*.

This term comes from the verb *kenoō* in Philippians 2:7, which says that in His incarnation Christ "emptied himself" (ESV). Probably the best way to understand this self-emptying is that in taking on a human nature and living among us, Christ relinquished the status, honor, and privilege He deserved as the Son of God, in order to serve us and secure our salvation. It is a powerful reminder that the incarnation was costly to our Lord. Think of that whenever you celebrate Christmas.

Jesus Christ's incarnation reminds us that He is an utterly unique person. The next term considers this critical issue more closely.

14 The Hypostatic Union

Who is Jesus Christ? One is hard-pressed to think of a more important question. Many have tried to fit Jesus into their particular worldview, and in doing so have tragically misunderstood who He is. There has therefore been a plethora of false teaching about Jesus since He walked the earth, even among professing Christians. In contrast, orthodox Christians have carefully summarized the Bible's teaching on the person of Christ in the doctrine of the hypostatic union. There are three key elements in this doctrine.

The first is the full deity of Christ. The Bible insists that Jesus Christ is fully God. He is explicitly called "God" in several places (e.g., John 1:1, 18; 20:28; Titus 2:13; Heb. 1:8). He has divine attributes, such as omniscience (John 16:20; 21:17), omnipotence (Matt. 8:26–27; cf. Ps. 107:28–29), omnipresence (Matt. 18:20; 28:20; Rom. 8:10), and eternity (John 1:1; 8:58). Divine titles are ascribed to Him (e.g., "Son of God," John 5:18; "I Am," John 8:58; "Alpha and Omega," Rev. 22:13). He performs divine acts, such as creating (John 1:3), sustaining all things (Col. 1:17), forgiving sins (Mark 2:1–12; Acts 5:31), granting salvation and eternal life (John 3:16; Acts 4:12; Rom. 10:12–17), raising the dead (John 5:21; 6:40; 11:1–44), and exercising final judgment (John 5:19–29; Acts 10:42). He is identified with Yahweh in the Old Testament (cf. John 12:40–41 with Isa. 6:1–10). He receives from human beings what is appropriate for only God to receive, such as worship (Matt. 14:33; 28:9, 17; Heb. 1:6; Rev. 5:8–12), prayer (Acts 7:59–60; 9:1–17; 1 Cor. 1:2), and trust for salvation (Acts 10:42–43; 16:31; Rom. 10:8–13). It is no exaggeration to say that if Jesus is not fully divine, then the Christian faith is blasphemous.

> **IT IS NO EXAGGERATION TO SAY THAT IF JESUS IS NOT FULLY DIVINE, THEN THE CHRISTIAN FAITH IS BLASPHEMOUS.**

The second key element of the hypostatic union is the full humanity of Christ. While affirming His deity, the Bible insists on His full humanity at the very same time. He Himself acknowledged His own humanity (Matt. 4:3–4; John 8:40) as did those who knew Him (Acts 2:22; Mark 6:1–6). The New Testament writers affirm His humanity (1 Tim. 2:5; John 1:14; Gal. 4:4; 1 Cor. 15:21), and John warns of the seriousness of denying it (1 John 4:2–3). He was born like us (Luke 2:7), grew up like us (Luke 2:40, 47), ate, drank, and slept like us (Matt. 8:23–24; 4:2; John 4:6; 19:28), experienced the whole range of emotions like us (Matt. 26:38; 8:10; 9:36; John 11:35; 12:27; Mark 3:5), was tempted like us (Matt. 4:1–11; Heb. 4:15), and even physically died like us (Luke 23). Without Jesus' full humanity, He could not be our faithful high priest who dealt with our sin on our behalf (Heb. 2:14–18), nor could He be the true Son of David and thus our messianic deliverer in fulfillment of prophecy (Rom. 1:2–3; cf. Matt. 1 and Luke 3), nor could He be the second Adam, the paradigm for redeemed humanity (1 Cor. 15:45–49; Rom. 5:12–21).

The third key element of the hypostatic union is the reality that Jesus' divine and human natures are united in His one person. The Greek word *hypostasis* was the term used in the early church for the person of Christ—hence "hypostatic union." Because Scripture always presents Christ as one person, those two natures are genuinely united in His one person; He is not divided into two people, a divine Jesus and a human Jesus. Yet, because Scripture upholds the integrity of those two natures as complete, they are not mixed together into some hybrid nature, neither fully human nor fully divine.

In sum, the doctrine of the hypostatic union maintains that, as a result of His incarnation, Jesus Christ has both a fully divine and a fully human nature, which are forever united in His one person without any mixture, change, or separation. This biblical doctrine was formally affirmed in the *Chalcedonian Creed* of 451, a creed embraced by all orthodox Christians up to the present day. The creed sought to address the challenges of various *Christological heresies* (false teachings about the person of Christ) that had arisen up to that point.

What are some of those heresies? Several of them opposed the true deity of Christ. For example, the *Ebionites* were an early Jewish-Christian sect that viewed Jesus only as a human Messiah endowed with special divine power. Far more significant was *Arianism*, which claimed that Christ was the first and greatest created being who, though God-like, was not truly God. Other heresies have rejected Christ's true humanity. For example, *docetism* believed that human flesh was inherently evil and thus incompatible with Christ's deity. They therefore denied that Christ was human at all, insisting that He only seemed to be human (the name comes from the Greek *dokeō*, "to seem or appear"). More subtly, *Apollinarianism* denied Christ's full humanity as it asserted that the divine Christ took on a human body but not a human spirit. And then some heresies denied the unity of these two complete natures in Christ's one person. *Nestorianism*, for instance, so downplayed the union of the two complete natures that it ended up treating Jesus like two people (one human, one divine). At the opposite end of the spectrum, *monophysitism* (or *Eutychianism*, named after a prominent advocate) so stressed the union of the two natures that it effectively merged the two natures into one divinely-dominated nature.

While the careful formulation of the doctrine of the hypostatic union is noteworthy, how much does it really matter after all? Isn't it enough just to believe in and love Jesus? That's crucial, to be sure, but one must in fact believe in and love the real Jesus. John affirms that one who gets the person of Christ wrong—whether in His deity or humanity—actually opposes Him and is excluded from a relationship with God (1 John 2:22–23; 4:2–3; 5:5). There are very good reasons for this, some of which we saw earlier. But consider two more. First, Christ is the mediator between God and humans (1 Tim. 2:5). In our union with Him in His full humanity, He brings us to God; in His identity as truly divine, He brings God to us; and in the unity of both natures in His person, He fully reconciles us to God. Second, Christ is the sufficient sacrifice for our sins, but only as fully human can He take the place of human beings, and only as God can He fully satisfy the penalty for humanity's sins. This sufficient sacrifice depends not only on the hypostatic union but also on His sinless life, a doctrine to which we now turn.

 ## 15   The Sinlessness of Christ

Often when we think about Christ's work of salvation, we think immediately of His death on the cross. But we must not skip over an important part of Jesus' story between His incarnation and death: His sinless life. The sinlessness of Christ means that Christ was not sinful in any way, nor did He ever sin; instead, He was perfectly righteous. The Bible clearly teaches this. Jesus Himself repeatedly affirmed His perfect obedience to the Father (John 8:29; 14:30–31; 15:10), and He is often called the "Holy One" or "Righteous One" (Acts 2:27; 3:14; 4:30; 7:52; 13:35; 1 Peter 3:18). Indeed, Jesus "knew no sin" (2 Cor. 5:21) because "in him there is no sin" (1 John 3:5 ESV), nor did He ever commit sin (1 Peter 2:22). He is the morally perfect, unblemished sacrifice for our sins (1 Peter 1:19; Heb. 9:14) and the "holy, innocent, unstained" high priest (Heb. 7:26 ESV) who offers that sacrifice. No wonder Jesus could confidently challenge His enemies in John 8:46 with the question: "Which one of you convicts me of sin?" (ESV).

Christ's sinlessness includes His very nature as a human being. Because all human beings have descended from Adam and Eve, we are all born with original sin—the sinful guilt and corruption inherited from Adam and Eve since the Fall (see **Original Sin**). But Jesus Christ is the one exception to this rule. He inherited neither Adam's guilt nor His corruption. We saw earlier that, in effecting Jesus' virgin birth, the Holy Spirit kept Jesus from inheriting original sin. Had Jesus inherited Adam's sinful guilt and corruption, He would not have been sinless.

Even though Jesus did not have a corrupt human nature, He still faced real temptation. Hebrews 4:15 insists that Jesus "in every respect has been tempted as we are, yet without sin" (ESV). Indeed, His earthly ministry both began with a temptation (Matt. 4:1–11) and came to a close with another (Matt. 26:36–46). Like the first Adam, who was tempted without a corrupt nature and yet failed, Jesus was the second Adam who was similarly tempted but triumphed. But this raises a question. Since Adam could (and did) sin, could Jesus also have sinned (even though He did not)? The doctrine of Christ's *impeccability* states that the person of Christ could not have sinned, despite being genuinely tempted. While some have argued that Christ could have sinned had He so chosen (*peccability*), most Christians have rightly affirmed Christ's impeccability. After all, the person of Christ is also fully God, and God cannot sin. Yet, in facing His temptations in His humanity, He provided a pattern for us to follow, and in never succumbing to those temptations, He experienced their full brunt.

But how does Jesus' sinlessness and impeccability square with His full humanity? After all, to err is human, isn't it? Is a sinless Jesus a truly human Jesus? These questions, and the assumption behind them, are wrongheaded. God did not create human beings as sinful, corrupt, and guilty creatures; in the Garden before the Fall, Adam and Eve were morally innocent. Further, when God completes His redemptive work in believers' lives at Christ's return, they will no longer be sinful, corrupt, and guilty. Instead they will be perfectly righteous and will live morally pure lives forever, having been conformed to the image of the sinless one, our Lord Jesus (Rom. 8:29). We might say, then, that sinful human beings fall short of what it means to be really human in God's design and plan. Jesus, as the true image of God (Col. 1:15; 2 Cor. 4:4), is the pattern for what it means to be truly human, and we are most human when we are most like Him.

But does Christ's sinless life really matter that much? Consider three important reasons why it does. First, Jesus in His sinless life provides the quintessential example for how we should live (Matt. 11:29; John 13:12–17; Phil. 2:5; 1 Peter 2:21; 1 John 2:5–6). And we should bear in mind that He provides this example precisely as a man who relies on the Father and Spirit every step of the way, just as we should. Second, Jesus' righteous life is the basis for our righteous status as believers. He was perfectly righteous in His life and was the beloved Son in whom the Father was well pleased (Matt. 3:17; 9:35). By faith we are united to Him when we are saved (see **Union with Christ**). As a result, His perfectly righteous status becomes ours (see **Justification**), and like Him we become God's beloved children as well. Finally, the Bible makes clear the principle that our sin can only be paid by an acceptable sacrifice, and to be acceptable that sacrifice must be pure. In His death on the cross, Jesus was that pure, sinless sacrifice for our sins (1 Peter 1:18–19; 3:18; Heb. 7:26; 9:14). Without His sinless life, He could not have provided such an effective sacrifice. But His sacrifice was incredibly effective, as we will see next.

16 ➤➤ Atonement

One of the most widespread symbols of Christianity is the cross. At first blush, this might seem rather strange if you know anything about Roman history. In ancient Rome, the cross represented crucifixion—a horrible, excruciating, humiliating form of execution for criminals. And yet the earliest Christians, taking their cue from the New Testament (Gal. 6:14; 1 Cor. 1:17–31), embraced this symbol. The reason is readily apparent: it represents Christ's death on the cross, which is at the heart of the gospel message. In summarizing the gospel message, Paul succinctly captures why Christ's death is so vital to the faith: "Christ died for our sins in accordance with the Scriptures" (1 Cor. 15:3 ESV).

We call this the atonement. This doctrine refers to Christ's work of resolving the central problem of humanity's sin and its dreadful effects. Christians have differed over the centuries in how to understand the precise nature of Christ's atoning work. Various atonement theories have therefore been proposed, each focusing on different objects of Christ's atoning work.

Certain theories have focused on the forces of evil as the object of the atonement. In some way, the atonement defeats the forces of evil that enslave or oppress sinful human beings. One ancient example is the *ransom theory*. This view assumes that Satan owned all fallen human beings. If we were to be freed from his clutches, a ransom price must be paid—and Christ's death was the ransom price Satan demanded. Christ provided that ransom and freed us, but neither death nor Satan could hold Him and Satan was thus defeated. Another theory, *recapitulation*, maintained that Christ defeated the oppressive power of sin and death bequeathed to us from Adam. He did this by reversing the curse of sin and death in His perfect incarnation, life, death, and resurrection, thereby becoming the Second Adam who creates a new, redeemed humanity in Himself. The *Christus victor theory*, broader than the first two, simply affirms that Christ's death on the cross constituted His victory over sin, Satan, and death.

A second group of atonement theories focuses on the effect of the atonement on human beings. According to these, the atonement in some sense changes our perception of God and sin so that we can be reconciled with Him. The *moral influence theory*, for example, sees Christ's death on the cross as a powerful demonstration of God's love toward us, a love that prompts us to love God in return. Similarly, the *example theory* sees Christ as the quintessential example of a godly man, a man thoroughly committed to obeying God, even at the expense of His own life. His example inspires us to follow the same path of committed obedience to the Lord and to receive forgiveness from Him. A more complex view is the *moral government theory*. It conceives of God as the ruler of the universe. As a ruler He has the power to relax His law and pardon us from the punishment our sin deserves. But if He simply cancels all punishment, sin will flourish unchecked in His universe. Christ's death therefore provides a deterrent, a powerful display of God's just punishment against lawbreak-ers. Sinners who wisely heed the cross's warning will turn from their sin to God for pardon; those who don't will face judgment.

MOST PROTESTANT EVANGELICALS RIGHTLY START WITH PENAL-SUBSTITUTION AS CENTRAL TO THE ATONEMENT.

A third set of atonement theories is directed toward God Himself. These maintain that our sin is an affront to God's character, and that affront must be satisfied. The *satisfaction theory* insists that God's dignity and honor have been insulted by our sin. That insult must be satisfied with a suitable compensation. Since God's majestic dignity is infinite, the compensation must be similarly infinite; yet because it is our sin, the compensation must be fulfilled by a man. Only Jesus Christ, who is both infinite God and fully human, can meet that satisfaction by His death on the cross on our behalf. The *penal-substitutionary theory* is similar, but it refines the satis-faction theory in an important way. It is God's holy *justice* that must be satisfied, and if it is to be satisfied, then sin's penalty must be paid. In love, however, God sent His Son to die on the cross to atone for our sins. As man Christ takes our place on the cross (substitution), and as God He fully satisfies the just penalty (penal) for our sins so we don't have to face it ourselves. By faith our sins are thereby paid in full and we are reconciled to God.

Which theory is correct? In truth, the Bible's teaching on the atonement is rich and complex, encompassing many elements of theories mentioned earlier. Yet our fundamental problem as sinners is our alienation from the living God due to our sin. This is why most Protestant evangelicals rightly start with penal-substitution as central to the atonement. Here's why. Scripture stresses that Christ's death on the cross was a sacrifice (Isa. 53; Heb. 9–10) whereby He bore sin's penalty (Gal. 3:10–14; Col. 2:13–15). In particular, as a substitutionary sacrifice, He took our sins upon Himself (Isa. 53:6; 2 Cor. 5:21; Gal. 3:13; 1 Peter 2:24). In doing so, God's righteous wrath— that we deserved—was fully satisfied and turned away from believers; this is called *propitiation* (Rom. 3:21–26; Heb. 2:17). Consequently, believers are completely forgiven of their sins (Eph. 1:7; Col. 2:13–14). What's more, they are reconciled to God, moving them from enemies to beloved children (Col. 1:21–22; Rom. 5:6–11; 2 Cor. 5:18–21).

Beyond dealing with our fundamental problem with God, the cross also defeats the forces of evil and, of course, affects human beings. Although God owes Satan nothing, Christ's death was a ransom in the sense that it cost God dearly to free us from sin (Matt. 20:28; Eph. 1:7; 1 Cor. 6:20; Rom. 6). In addition, the cross's apparent defeat in fact marked a great victory over Satan and his minions (1 John 3:8; Col. 2:15; cf. Gen. 3:15). Moreover, sin and death itself were defeated in the death and resurrection of the second Adam, who represents redeemed humanity (Rom. 5–6). Further, the cross provides an example for believers to follow Jesus faithfully even if it means suffering (1 Peter 2:21).

The Bible's rich and complex picture of Christ's atoning work helps explain not only why Christians have put so much emphasis on it, but also why they have debated its meaning in the various atonement theories. Christians have also debated two other matters related to the cross. The first of these is the *extent* (or *intent*) of the atonement. That is, did Christ die only for the ones He has chosen for salvation throughout time (the *elect*), or did He die to make the atonement available to every human being? Those who hold to *limited atonement* (or *particular redemption*) maintain the former, that Christ died for the elect only—and actually secured their redemption. Those who hold to *unlimited atonement* affirm the latter, that Christ's work on the cross made salvation universally available for anyone who will accept it. This debate is part of the larger debate between Calvinism and Arminianism (see **Calvinism**).

Second, Christians also debate the *descent into hell*. That is, did Christ literally descend into hell between His death and resurrection? This doctrine is included in later editions of the Apostles' Creed, and advocates appeal to texts like Ephesians 4:9–10 and 1 Peter 3:19–20 to support the view. But interpretation of these texts is highly disputed. Other Christians deny the descent into hell because no biblical text clearly supports it and because Jesus promised the thief on the cross in Luke 23:43 (ESV) that "today" He would join Jesus in "Paradise" (i.e., heaven).

When thinking about Christ's atoning work on the cross, we must remember one final point. The New Testament makes clear that the cross cannot be isolated from Christ's resurrection (1 Cor. 15:3–4). The cross saves because Christ was raised (1 Cor. 15:12–19; Rom. 4:23–25). We therefore need to consider the resurrection more closely.

17 The Exaltation of Christ

Actually, the resurrection ushered in the exaltation of Christ. This refers to the phase of Christ's incarnational work that began with His resurrection and will culminate in His return and eternal reign. It is an exaltation because Christ receives the status of glory and honor He so richly deserves. It presupposes the *humiliation of Christ*, the earlier phase of Christ's ministry in which He was born of the virgin Mary, lived humbly (and sinlessly) among us, suffered a humiliating death on the cross, and was buried. The key text here is Philippians 2:5–11, which teaches both Christ's humiliation in becoming a human being and dying on the cross and His subsequent exaltation when God "highly exalted him and bestowed on him the name that is above every name" (v. 9 ESV). There are several elements of Christ's exaltation.

The first is the *resurrection of Christ*. This doctrine affirms that Christ returned from the dead with a glorified human body. The Scriptures insist that Christ's resurrection is a historical fact—so important that to deny it is to deny the faith itself (1 Cor. 15:12–19). Indeed, as mentioned above, it is the necessary twin of the cross, and together they constitute the very heart of the gospel (1 Cor. 15:1–4; Rom. 5:9–10).

Why is the resurrection so essential? For one thing, it ensures that our sins have been forgiven and that we have been justified (Rom. 4:25; 1 Cor. 15:17), probably because it confirms that Christ's sacrifice was acceptable to God. It also confirms who Jesus really is: the powerful Son of God who will rule over all (Rom. 1:4; Acts 17:31). Moreover, the resurrection guarantees that believers will also be similarly resurrected with perfected human bodies at Christ's return (1 Cor. 15:12–58; 6:14; 2 Cor. 4:14; John 11:25). Further, the resurrection is the basis for the new spiritual life we have in Jesus Christ (Rom. 6:1–14; Eph. 2:5–6; 1 Peter 1:3). Finally, the resurrection ensures that God will complete all He has pledged in His redemption plan (1 Cor. 15:19–28). Because He has risen, believers have every reason to be confidently hopeful and steadfast in our present labors (1 Cor. 15:58).

Another element of Christ's exaltation is His *ascension* and *session*. After His resurrection appearances, Christ was lifted bodily into heaven (*ascension*), where He was seated at God's right hand (*session*) until He comes again (Luke 24:50–51; Acts 1:9–11; 2:32–36; Matt. 26:64; Heb. 1:3; 10:12–13). He is now in the place of honor that He deserves (Acts 2:33; Phil. 2:9). In addition, He is in the place of authority; by right and power He is king over all. Already He is ruling from heaven (Eph. 1:20–21; 1 Peter 3:22), although His rule will not be fully realized in the world until He returns (Heb. 10:12–13). Nevertheless, His universal rule over all things, including His most implacable enemies, is inevitable (1 Cor. 15:25–26; Phil. 2:9–11), and believers should always bear this in mind in the face of the evils of this present world.

HE IS ALREADY EXALTED, AND PEOPLE WHO WISH TO IGNORE THAT REALITY WILL EVENTUALLY BE FORCED TO FACE IT.

From the right hand of the Father, Jesus also continues to work on behalf of His people. On the day of Pentecost He sent His Spirit to indwell believers (Acts 2:33). He continues to intercede to the Father on our behalf (Heb. 7:23–25; Rom. 8:34). And He is consistently at work in the church through His Spirit, building His church (Matt. 16:18), leading her as the head (Eph. 1:20–23; 5:23–24; Col. 1:18), gifting her (Eph. 4:7–11), cleansing and nourishing her (Eph. 5:23–30), and preparing a place for her in heaven (John 14:1–3).

Christ's exaltation culminates in His Second Coming— His powerful return to earth in glory and triumph. We will consider this doctrine in more detail in the final chapter. Suffice it to say here that when Jesus returns to earth, every knee will bow and every tongue will confess that He is Lord (Phil. 2:10). He is already exalted, and people who wish to ignore that reality will eventually be forced to face it. Those of us who already bow the knee to our exalted Lord, in contrast, eagerly look forward to "our blessed hope, the appearing of the glory of our great God and Savior Jesus Christ" (Titus 2:13 ESV).

5

THE DOCTRINE OF THE HOLY SPIRIT
(Pneumatology)

 **The Person of the Holy Spirit**

The very names of the first two persons of the Trinity, God the Father and God the Son, remind us that they are persons with whom we relate. But the name of the third person, God the Holy Spirit, seems different—more abstract, less personal. And certainly there is something elusive and mysterious about Him (John 3:3–8). Perhaps this is the reason some Christians inadvertently refer to Him as "it" from time to time, and others are tempted to think of Him as little more than God's power. But this kind of thinking mischaracterizes the person of the Holy Spirit, who as the third person of the Trinity is both fully divine and fully personal, just like the

85

other two persons of the Godhead. In order to understand who the Spirit is more fully, we need to look more closely at both His personality and His deity.

When thinking about the personality of the Holy Spirit, it is important to remember first of all that He truly is a person. He is not some force, nor is He simply a metaphor for God's power. The Bible is quite clear about this important point. For example, the Spirit has various attributes regularly associated with personality, such as His own mind (Rom. 8:27), emotions (Eph. 4:30), and will (1 Cor. 12:11). In addition, He displays self-awareness, referring to Himself as "I" in Acts 13:2. He also is called the "Helper" (or Comforter) who continues the work that Jesus did in the disciples' lives (John 14:16–17, 26). Further, He interacts with other persons as a person. He teaches (John 14:26), speaks (Acts 8:29), intercedes (Rom. 8:26), testifies (John 15:26), commands (Acts 10:19–20), guides (John 16:13), and commissions (Acts 13:2–4). He also can be lied to (Acts 5:3), grieved (Eph. 4:30), blasphemed (Matt. 12:31), and insulted (Heb. 10:29).

The Spirit is not just a person; He is God, sharing the totality of the divine being with the Father and the Son. This explains why the Spirit is so closely associated with the other two divine persons in Scripture (Matt. 3:16–17; 28:19; 1 Peter 1:2; 1 Cor. 12:4–6; 2 Cor. 13:14). It also explains passages like Acts 5:2–4, which explicitly refers to the Holy Spirit as God when it equates lying to the Spirit with lying to God, and Hebrews 10:15–17, which identifies a quote from Yahweh in Jeremiah

31:31–34 as a quote from the Holy Spirit. The Spirit's deity is further supported by the various divine attributes ascribed to Him, such as eternality (Heb. 9:14), divine power (Luke 1:35), divine omniscience (1 Cor. 2:10–11), omnipresence (Ps. 139:7–10), and holiness (Rom. 1:4). He also performs divine actions, like creating (Gen. 1:2; Ps. 104:29–30), regenerating (Titus 3:5), inspiring Scripture (2 Peter 1:20–21), and effecting the virgin birth of Christ (Luke 1:35).

While orthodox Christians have universally agreed on the deity and personality of the Holy Spirit as the third person of the Trinity, they have disagreed on the nature of the relationship the Spirit enjoys with the Father and Son. This has been called the *filioque controversy*. This controversy became acute during the Middle Ages between the Eastern Greek-speaking church and the Western Latin-speaking church, culminating in the formal separation of the two in 1054. Essentially the debate centered on whether the Spirit "proceeds" from both the Father and the Son (Western church), or from the Father alone (Eastern church). During the medieval period, the Western church added the phrase "and the Son" (*filioque* in Latin) to the Nicene Creed's statement on the Holy Spirit, which reads, "I believe in the Holy Spirit, the Lord and giver of life, who proceeds from the Father [*and the Son*]." The Eastern church found the addition, and the theology behind it, unacceptable. The debate itself is not as esoteric as it may sound, for it relates directly to how one understands the relationship between the three persons of the Godhead.

Given what we have seen about the person of the Holy Spirit, the Nicene Creed (both in Eastern and Western versions) has good reason to go on to say that the Spirit "together with the Father and the Son is worshiped and glorified." We have good reason to follow the Creed's lead. As we contemplate, in the next entry, the incredible works the Spirit does in our lives as believers, remember that it is God the Holy Spirit—the fully divine third person of the Trinity—who is at work in our lives in these wonderful ways.

19 The Works of the Holy Spirit

Some jobs require so many different tasks that it can be really difficult to write a job description for them. We can feel the same way when trying to articulate the Holy Spirit's "job description," for the works of the Holy Spirit include all the many things the third person of the Trinity does both in the world and in our lives. Here we will attempt to consider many of these—although this job description will not be exhaustive.

The Spirit clearly works on a global scale, affecting history and the world in general. For example, He was involved with the Father and the Son in creating the world (Gen. 1:2; Ps. 104:29–30). He was also active in revealing God, both in empowering prophets to prophesy (e.g., Num. 11:25–30; Luke

1:67) and in inspiring Scripture (2 Peter 1:20–21). He was active too throughout the life of Christ, from His virgin birth (Luke 1:35) through His baptism (Luke 3:21–22) and ministry (Luke 4:1, 16–21; Matt. 12:28) to His death and resurrection (Heb. 9:14; Rom. 8:11; 1 Peter 3:18). He is even active in convicting the fallen world of humanity, exposing its sinfulness and skewed standards of righteousness and judgment (John 16:8–11).

In addition to His global works, the Spirit is active in the lives of believers as well. If Christ's work is central for accomplishing the salvation of believers, the Spirit's work is also critical for applying Christ's saving work to believers. And if the salvation Christ accomplished takes us from conversion to glorification (see chapter 8 for more on these terms), the Spirit is also active in our lives all along the way. Consequently, let's consider what the Spirit does in applying Christ's work of salvation from the beginning of our Christian lives until He takes us home.

At the very outset of our Christian life the Spirit regenerates the believer, imparting spiritual life to those who are spiritually dead in sin (John 3:1–8; Titus 3:5–6; cf. Eph. 2:1–2; John 6:63; 2 Cor. 3:6). This work changes our very nature and enables us to turn to Christ (see **Conversion**). When we are saved, we are also baptized in the Spirit (1 Cor. 12:13; cf. Matt. 3:11; John 1:33; Acts 1:5; 11:16). This work is both controversial and complex, but here we will simply say that it involves uniting us with Christ and His body and receiving the Spirit in our lives (see **Spirit Baptism**).

When the Spirit comes into our lives in Spirit baptism, He stays with us forever thereafter. This is called *indwelling*, a term that comes from Scripture's teaching that the Spirit of God dwells in each believer (John 14:16–17; Rom. 8:9–11; Gal. 4:6; 2 Tim. 1:14), and it evokes the remarkable image that each of us is His temple (1 Cor. 6:19). Because He is God, the Spirit is present everywhere, but with believers He is present in a meaningful way. We should therefore not think of indwelling in mere spatial terms, any more than we think of location when we talk about a "close friend" or spouse who is a "part of me." The language is relational, personal, even intimate. All believers have Him, and He has us, even as He binds us to the Son and the Father (Rom. 8:9–11; Gal. 4:6). Our relationship with Him is the basis for all the other works He does in our lives. And because Jesus insisted that He will be with us forever (John 14:16), that relationship is permanent. He is always with you and will never leave you!

The Spirit's permanent presence with believers means that they will always belong to God and that their salvation is eternally secure. This is called the Spirit's work of *sealing* the believer. The term comes from the metaphor of the Spirit as a "seal" (2 Cor. 1:21–22; Eph. 1:13–14; 4:30), which suggests that the Spirit's presence is like a seal signifying that believers belong to God and guaranteeing the completion of their salvation. Similarly, the Spirit is called a "down payment" (2 Cor. 1:21–22; 5:5; Eph. 1:14 CSB) and the firstfruits (Rom. 8:23), metaphors picking up on the same idea as the "seal" metaphor.

The Spirit's constant and secure indwelling presence also means He is active throughout our Christian lives. He does, in fact, regularly *intercede* for us as we pray to our Father in heaven (Rom. 8:26–27). His intercessions for us are always effective because, being God, He perfectly knows God's will for us and always prays in accord with it. This is why it's so critical for us to pray in the Spirit (Eph. 6:18) and according to God's will (1 John 5:14–15; Matt. 26:39); otherwise, our prayers will be little more than ineffective articulations of our desires (see James 4:2–3). Even more broadly, the Spirit is consistently working in our lives to sanctify us (see **Sanctification**), setting us apart to God (1 Cor. 6:11), making us increasingly more like Christ in our daily lives (1 Peter 1:2; 2 Thess. 2:13; Rom. 8:4), and producing His fruit of godliness in our walk with Him (Gal. 5:22–23). One of the means He uses to sanctify us is through God's Word. In this connection, the Spirit *illuminates* believers as they read and study Scripture (1 Cor. 2:9–16; 2 Cor. 4:4–6). In this wonderful work, the Spirit helps believers understand, appreciate, and apply Scripture to their lives. Together the Word and Spirit are a powerful team in a believer's walk.

At times throughout their lives, Christians can also be *filled* with the Spirit. In this work, the Spirit empowers believers beyond their own capacity. Sometimes that empowerment involves a specific task or situation, as when people prophesy (Luke 1:41–42, 67) or proclaim God's Word powerfully (Acts 2:4; 4:8, 31). Old Testament believers experienced this as well when the Spirit came upon them (Num. 11:25; Judg. 14:5–6; 1 Sam. 10:10). Sometimes the Spirit's empowerment can characterize a believer's life as a whole (Acts 6:3–5; 11:24). In these cases, believers so consistently submit to the direction of the Spirit and rely on His power that He produces true godly character in their lives. This is why Paul commands us to be filled with the Spirit (Eph. 5:18–21) and to walk by the Spirit (Gal. 5:16–18, 22–25) rather than to "grieve" Him (Eph. 4:30) or "quench" Him (1 Thess. 5:19). Filling in this sense is absolutely essential to growing in godliness and producing the fruit of the Spirit (Gal. 5:22–25) and thus is inextricably related to His work of sanctifying us.

It should be clear by now that the Spirit's works in the world and in our lives are extensive—and wonderful. And the list of the Spirit's works mentioned here is not even exhaustive! But it would be negligent if we did not mention one other work of the Spirit. Given the controversy surrounding it, this work deserves an entry all its own.

20 ⟫ Spiritual Gifts

Some matters spur intense interest and controversy among Christians. One is the topic of spiritual gifts. We will consider why that is presently, but let's begin with a definition. Spiritual gifts are abilities graciously given to every believer by the

Holy Spirit to serve one another in the church. The New Testament lists spiritual gifts in five places (1 Cor. 12:6–8; 12:28; Rom. 12:6–8; Eph. 4:11; 1 Peter 4:10–11). None of these lists is the same. Some gifts appear repeatedly (e.g., teaching), while others are presented only once (e.g., giving in Rom. 12:8). And the gifts may even overlap at times; for example, Peter simply lists speaking and serving gifts (1 Peter 4:10–11), which are closer to categories than specific gifts. All of this suggests that the gift lists are intended as representative and illustrative rather than exhaustive.

What are some important features of spiritual gifts? First, they are gracious gifts from the triune God, specifically through the Spirit (1 Cor. 12:7–11). This is why they are called *charismata* (grace gifts) and *pneumatikos* (matters pertaining to the Spirit) in the Greek New Testament. They are therefore not mere natural abilities (even though they may sometimes be related to natural abilities), for it is the Spirit who grants them to believers and empowers them to produce spiritual fruit among God's people. Neither should they be a source of pride. Whatever giftedness we have has been granted to us by the Spirit and used by Him.

Second, every believer has at least one spiritual gift, and no one has them all (1 Peter 4:10; 1 Cor. 12:4–7). To those who think they have nothing to offer God's people, this feature is an apt reminder that they should abandon such notions, because the church needs them. And to busy ministry leaders tempted to think their ministry depends on them, it is a reminder that they need the help of other Christians to accomplish God's work. Although everyone has a spiritual gift, this does not mean everyone is equally gifted. One believer might have a particular gift to a greater degree than others with the same gift (Acts 18:24; 1 Cor. 14:28). Or another believer may have a combination of several gifts, while others have only one. Yet in neither case does greater giftedness bequeath to its bearer any superiority or special status, for each believer is a vital member of the body of Christ, and the health of the whole body depends on the effective functioning of each part (1 Cor. 12:21–26). Besides, highly gifted Christians cannot claim they have earned anything, since it is the Spirit who sovereignly distributes the gifts as He determines (1 Cor. 4:7; 12:11).

Third, spiritual gifts are about strengthening others in the body, not about one's personal self-fulfillment. Christians sometimes fall into the trap of thinking that exercising their gifts is about them. True, effectively ministering one's gift can be fulfilling, but that is only a side effect, for the gifts are given for the "common good" of the body of Christ (1 Cor. 12:7), which grows toward Christlikeness "when each part is working properly" (Eph. 4:16 ESV). Since each believer's gift is given for the sake of the body, discovering that gift is best done in the context of the Christian community. While personal introspection may be of some benefit for discovering one's gift, the observations of our fellow believers in the body are even more beneficial. After all, they are typically well-situated to see how the Spirit is using someone in the actual life of the church to produce spiritual fruit.

Finally, as indicated earlier, the spiritual gifts are contro-versial. One of the greatest areas of controversy concerns the miraculous nature of some of the gifts. This category includes gifts like working miracles, healing, speaking in tongues, and prophecy. Do such gifts continue today, or are they limited to the apostolic era? Many Christians would insist that all these gifts continue in the church today, and so they are called *continuationists*. They point out that no biblical text clearly teaches that miraculous gifts have ceased, and they attest that believers continue to experience them. To be sure, continu-ationists differ with one another over the emphasis they place on the miraculous gifts. For example, those who are part of Pentecostal and charismatic churches stress these gifts, affirm-ing their necessity for a healthy church. But other continu-ationists are more cautious about their use, acknowledging that God does continue to grant these gifts but doubting that He does so as widely as charismatics and Pentecostals assume.

In contrast to continuationism, some Christians known as *cessationists* insist that the miraculous gifts ceased in the apostolic era or shortly thereafter. They maintain that God gave these gifts in connection with the apostles to testify to the truth of the gospel message in order to help found the church. As such, cessationists typically call the miraculous gifts *sign gifts*. Cessationists stress at least two theological points. First, they point to the uniqueness of the apostolic era. The apostles were given to establish the church (Eph. 2:20), which is why the office no longer exists. The apostles were marked by miraculous signs (2 Cor. 12:12), as was the era of which they were a part (Heb. 2:2–4), establishing the truth of the gospel message they proclaimed. But once they passed off the scene, miraculous gifts faded, as is evident in church history. Second, cessationists point to the final and sufficient authority of the Bible. They maintain that if God continues to give direct revelation in prophecy and tongues, this ongoing revelation would bear the authority of God Himself and thus share equal authority with Scripture. It is therefore inconsistent for continuationists to insist that direct special revelation continues today while also affirming the final and sufficient authority of Scripture at the same time (as most do).

Regardless of one's view on the miraculous gifts, it cannot be denied that the Spirit continues to work powerfully in the life of each believer today. And He does this in no small measure through other believers, whom He has gifted according to His will. Each of us therefore has an important part to play in the Spirit's grand work. It is a tremendous blessing we should eagerly embrace.

6

THE DOCTRINE OF ANGELS, SATAN, AND DEMONS

(Angelology)

 **Angels**

Angels—everyone loves angels. They fly around protecting people in danger, and they are warm and fuzzy, helping people feel loved. Do I really need to understand this term? I already know what angels are and how to get them to work in my life—don't I? Actually, our familiarity with angels is one of the challenges; it is hard to separate what popular culture tells us about them and what Scripture reveals. It may surprise you to know that these two theological delivery systems differ greatly when it comes to angels, so let's look together at the theology of angels, what theologians refer to as Angelology.

Angels are created, spiritual beings who do not have physical bodies but are able to make judgments and possess intelligence. The Hebrew word *malak* and the Greek word *aggelos* point to the idea of a messenger. As created spiritual beings they have not existed eternally (Neh. 9:6; Ps. 148:2, 5). They are part of the "invisible" things God created (Col. 1:16).

When were they created? The Bible does not address that directly, but they may have been created on the first day, after the creation of heaven (Gen. 1:1; Job 38:4–7). So, if you are sitting in a coffee shop and your friend asks where you think angels come from, a good answer would be they were a special creation of God that occurred before the creation of humans (Gen. 1:1a; 2:1; John 1:3).

Angels are not corporeal, which means they don't have bodies the same way we as humans do. An Ecumenical Council that met in Nicaea in 784, however, declared angels have bodies of ether or light, pointing to Matthew 28:3 and Luke 2:9 for their support. A later Council, the Fourth Lateran Council in 1215, contradicted the earlier one and declared that angels are incorporeal and do not have bodies like we do (Ps. 104:4; Heb. 1:14). This is the prevailing understanding today, one that suggests they are simply spiritual beings. Angels are, however, real individual beings who are finite and spatial. It is just that their relationship to the space-time continuum is different from ours—sort of like Doctor Who but without the Tardis (Luke 8:30; Eph. 6:12).

Angels have personalities; they are able to make judgments

and possess intellectual knowledge (cf. Matt. 24:36; Gal. 3:16). They offer intelligent worship to God and possess emotions, too (Ps. 148:2; Luke 15:10). They are moral beings who know right from wrong and possess a will and, in the future, will be punished or rewarded for their actions (2 Tim. 2:26; 2 Peter 2:4; Jude 6). They have superhuman wisdom and strength but are not omniscient or omnipotent since they act in response to God's Word (Matt. 24:36; 2 Sam. 14:20; 1 Peter 1:12; Ps. 103:20; 2 Peter 2:11). Ultimately, angels are subservient to Christ; they are referred to as "his mighty angels" (2 Thess. 1:7 ESV; cf. 1 Peter 3:22; Col. 2:10). That can give us confidence as we wonder about our possible engagement with them.

As we mentioned earlier, popular culture delivers its own theology of angel-ness. So, here are a few details to consider the next time you watch a movie with angels as part of the story-line. There is no explicit reference confirming that angels as a whole are winged (but see the Seraphim in Isaiah 6:2, 6). Logically, then, it is not a necessary inference for all angels. Nor is there any definitive reference in regard to the belief that at birth each person is given a personal guardian angel that serves as their protector as they live (see Matthew 18:10 and Acts 12:15 for the two verses often misused for this view). While the scriptural support for personal guardian angels is lacking, there is strong scriptural witness in relation to their ministry in general (Heb. 1:14; Ps. 34:7). Angels do not have gender *per se* and are not able to procreate with humans (Matt. 22:28–30); there is no propagation among them, they do not die, and thus their numbers do not increase or decrease (Luke 20:34–36). This then also suggests that stories like Clarence's in *It's a Wonderful Life*, and the proverbial "when a bell rings an angel gets its wings," while enjoyable to watch, aren't supported scripturally. What becomes obvious is that the vast array of movies, television shows, books, and video games do not provide trustworthy information on the biblical purpose of angels and how we should relate to them. Let's conclude with addressing those two points: (a) angels' purpose and (b) our relation to them.

There are five overall purposes for angels. First, they were created to glorify God: "Praise him, all his angels; Praise him, all his hosts!" (Ps. 148:2 ESV), Second, their purpose is to serve God: "For by Him all things were created, both in the heavens and on earth, visible and invisible, whether thrones or dominions or rulers or authorities—all things have been created through Him and for Him" (Col. 1:16 NASB). Third, they are designed to learn God's wisdom and grace: "so that the multifaceted wisdom of God might now be made known through the church to the rulers and the authorities in the heavenly places" (Eph. 3:10 NASB). Fourth, they are tasked with reflecting God's attributes: "And one called out to another and said: 'Holy, Holy, Holy, is the LORD of hosts; the whole earth is full of His glory!'" (Isa. 6:3 NASB). Finally, in relation to us, their purpose is to minister to God's elect: "Are they not all ministering spirits, sent out to provide service for the sake of those who will inherit salvation?" (Heb. 1:14 NASB).

So, if these are their purposes, how are we to relate to

angels in a practical way? Obviously not the way popular culture suggests, though being aware of these depictions is a great way to open up spiritual conversations and be able to share a more theologically chastened understanding. First, we are not to venerate angels (Matt. 4:10). Second, we should always beware of fallen angels (2 Cor. 11:14; see **Demons**). Third, we ought to respect their service to God (2 Peter 2:10). Fourth, we must entertain strangers in a spirit of hospitality, as if they were angels (Heb. 13:2). Finally, we should be mindful that angels also observe us (1 Peter 1:12).

Satan

The juxtaposition of sacred and secular themes is a hallmark of country music. However, Satan rarely makes an appearance in lyrics. One exception is the 1979 Charlie Daniels Band song, "The Devil Went Down to Georgia," in which Satan tries to bargain for the soul of the fiddler Johnny. Folk beliefs about Satan permeate the theology of many church attenders; these everyday theological views influence people in ways formal teachings rarely do. So, let's clarify our theology in regard to Satan and see if we can spot any lingering folk religion that might have crept in while listening to our favorite genre of music—even if it's country.

Satan is the leader among the demons. He goes by many

names, including "prince of demons" (Matt. 12:24; Luke 11:15), "prince of this world" (John 12:31), "prince of the power of the air" (Eph. 2:2 ESV), "god of this age" (2 Cor. 4:4), "Satan" (Zech. 3:1; Rev. 12:9), "Devil" (Luke 4:2; Rev. 12:9), and "the evil one" (John 17:15; 1 John 5:18). He is not a mere literary trope or an impersonal force—he is a personal being.

The Hebrew word *satan* is often translated as "adversary," while the Greek word *satanas* is simply a transliteration of the original Hebrew term and maintains "adversary" as its primary referent. Satan's adversarial activity toward humanity is seen in the story of Job. In Job 1:6 and 2:1, the "sons of God" (ESV) present themselves before the Lord, and Satan is among them. He eventually carries on a conversation with God in which he maligns Job's character and asks to be allowed to test his devotion (1:11). God allows it but restricts his activity; he may not act beyond God's sovereign control (1:12; 2:6–7). In Zechariah 3:1–2, Satan is described as "standing at [God's] right hand to accuse [Joshua the high priest]" (ESV). Here he accuses the Lord's servant similar to what was seen in Job's story; but he remains subservient to God's sovereign, elective purpose.

Satan appears again in 1 Chronicles 21:1: "Satan rose up against Israel and incited David to take a census of Israel." Here Satan is the agent of David's sin. Even here the sinful circumstances related to the census are not beyond the control of God (2 Sam. 24:1). Theologically, it is important to include reflection on primary and secondary causes in seeking to understand God's providential work in the world, especially in relation to evil. This doctrine is known as *concurrence*— God's pervasive collaborative work with His creation. While some theologians make significant use of the doctrine of concursus, others find it less helpful.

The presentation of Satan in the New Testament follows closely what was seen in the Old Testament. The generic "accuser" in the Old Testament is now embroiled directly with Jesus (Matt. 4:10). Revelation 12:10 continues to reveal the primary and ongoing function of Satan as "the accuser." Paul's statement that "the God of peace will soon crush Satan under your feet" (Rom. 16:20), with its allusion to the "serpent" of Genesis 3:15, raises an important hermeneutical question: is the serpent in the garden of Eden Satan (Gen. 3:1)? John 8:44 seems to allude to the idea that Satan was the serpent (cf. 2 Cor. 11:3; 1 John 3:8), and Revelation 12:9 and 20:2 explicitly connect the two. So, while a full-blown doctrine of Satan is difficult to discern in Israel's scriptural tradition, canonically we can detect continuity between the way Satan works in the progress of revelation and that seen in the serpent of Genesis. Here we simply raise an important theological hermeneutical point: caution should be used when reading New Testament understandings back into the Old Testament passages (see **Theological Hermeneutics**).

Understanding what Satan means theologically requires attention to what Scripture reveals about his nature and identity. As for his nature, he possesses intellectual capacities since he is capable of deceiving and tempting individuals (2 Cor. 11:3;

Luke 4:1). He can express emotions such as wrath or pride (Rev. 12:12; 1 Tim. 3:6). He also has a will, since he can give commands or direct the activities of others (Luke 4:3, 9; Rev. 20:7–9). God will eventually judge him; thus he possesses culpability (2 Cor. 11:14–15; John 16:11). As for Satan's identity, he is a created being (Col. 1:16). More specifically, he is part of the originally created company of angels (Job 1:6–8; Matt. 25:41; Rev. 12:7). Some theologians refer to him as "a guardian cherub" (Ezek. 28:14); others recognize his prominence from his confrontation with the archangel Michael (Jude 9).

Though Satan is morally evil, he was originally created good (1 Tim. 4:4). He fell from his original heavenly estate as a guardian of God's glory (Jude 6; Ezek. 28:14) by rebelling against God and ultimately being banished to the earth (Ezek. 28:16–17; Isa. 14:12). (It should be noted that theologians debate whether Ezekiel 28 and Isaiah 14 can support such a fully developed doctrine of Satan at this early stage.) God was not the direct cause of Satan's sin; it arose from Satan's own free choice (James 1:13). God did permit this evil in order to produce a greater good. Even though Satan continues to oppose God's work in the world, God will ultimately triumph over Satan, evil, and death by (a) defeating sin (1 Cor. 15:25–26); (b) destroying his works (1 John 3:8); and (c) redeeming humanity (Rom. 5:20–21).

Why does this matter? Satan, though ultimately defeated, still works in various ways against human flourishing; therefore, we should always be aware of his devices. We may note a couple of analogies from his strategies in the New Testament: (a) hindering our ministry practice (1 Thess. 2:18); (b) inducing us to sin (Eph. 4:26–27); and (c) creating division within congregations due to a lack of forgiveness (2 Cor. 2:10–11). His plans, however, may be thwarted since he may be resisted (James 4:7; 1 Peter 5:8–9). His power over a person's life can be broken (Acts 26:18; Luke 22:32). His temptations in our life can be overcome (Matt. 4:1–11; James 1:14; 1 Cor. 10:13). We seek clarity on this theological term "in order that Satan might not outwit us. For we are not unaware of his schemes" (2 Cor. 2:11).

23 Demons

Demons make for epic villains in horror movies, whether Pazuzu in *The Exorcist* or Azazel in *Fallen*. However, horror movies are a poor place to develop your theology. The demon-possession subgenre, such as *The Exorcism of Emily Rose* or *Ouija: Origin of Evil*, create even more difficulties when trying to separate folk theology from biblically based theology. Having clear definitions in regard to demons provides us with tools to think theologically about popular culture—and the degree to which these genres are appropriate forms of entertainment.

Demons are angels who were originally created good but are now fallen and evil, since they followed their leader Satan in rebelling against God and now are aligned against His purposes in the world. Several Hebrew words are used to account for these beings. *Shed* is used in Deuteronomy 32:17 and Psalm 106:36–37 to indicate that some in Israel were sacrificing to "demons" or "false gods." *Ruah raah* occurs in Judges 9:23–24 and may be interpreted as an "evil spirit" (NASB), one sent by God. The idea of an "evil spirit" coming from the Lord is also present in other Old Testament passages (1 Sam. 16:14–15, 23; 18:10–11; 1 Kings 22:19–23). *Sair* appears in Leviticus 17:7 and is translated into English as "goat demons" (NASB; cf. Isa. 13:21; 34:14; 2 Chron. 11:15)—it probably points to indigenous cultic practices incompatible with the worship of the one God.

Daniel 10:13, with its phrase "the prince of the Persian kingdom," and 10:20, with its similar phrase "the prince of Persia," are understood by some to refer to territorial spirits, or demons given authority over broad geographical regions. In a contemporary setting, some Christians practice spiritual mapping whereby demons and demonic strongholds are identified and bound in the name of Jesus. The Daniel 10 passage is pointed to as justification for this practice. *Spiritual warfare* is an all-too-often ignored aspect of the Christian life, and intercessory prayer should be encouraged. Yet this passage is misused when it provides the sole justification for spiritual mapping. In Daniel 9:4–19, where Daniel's prayer is recorded, he does not follow the "binding of territorial spirits or fallen angels" approach. In the New Testament, the key passage on spiritual warfare is Ephesians 6:10–17, where the controlling verb is "to stand." Prayer is part of the larger context (6:18–20), but its nature differs from what's suggested by contemporary practitioners of spiritual mapping.

Demons are pervasive in the New Testament, with three terms accounting for most of the descriptors. *Daimonion* is most often translated as "demon," and occurs prominently in the Gospels (Matt. 9:33–34; Mark 1:34, 39; Luke 4:33, 35). *Pneuma*, when translated as "spirit," will have a delimiter in front of it when the context suggests malevolent beings in view: (a) "unclean spirits" (Acts 8:7 NASB) or (b) "evil spirits" (Acts 19:13). *Aggelos* in some contexts can refer to fallen angels (Jude 6).

Demons originated as good immaterial beings—all of God's creation is good—but they followed Satan in his revolt against God (1 Tim. 4:4a; Jude 6; 2 Peter 2:4; Col. 1:16). They possess traits associated with personal beings: (a) the ability to speak (Luke 4:33–34); (b) understand actions (Mark 1:23–24); (c) feel angst (Luke 8:28); and (d) choose (Luke 8:32). They are also evil beings in relation to humans, and they seek to: (a) deceive and lie (2 Cor. 11:14); (b) propagate false teaching (1 Tim. 4:1–2); (c) destroy human flourishing (Matt. 12:43–45); and (d) spread evil (Eph. 6:12). Thus they are powerful beings who can influence human cognition (2 Cor. 4:4) and patterns of embodiment (Luke 8:29).

One pressing question in regard to demons is: Can a Christian be *demon-possessed*? Theologians traditionally distinguish between (a) oppression, which refers to external influence by a demon, and (b) possession, which requires internal control of the person by a demon. Matthew 15:22 is one place where a person is described as "demon-possessed" (*daimonizomai*). The context suggests this is an appropriate translation. However, some prefer the alternative "demonized," since they don't think Christians can be "possessed." How should we think about this issue? Those in Christ belong to Christ—not to a demon (1 Cor. 3:23). The complete lordship of Jesus described in Acts 10:36 works against the claim that those in Christ can be possessed by demons, and it would be incompatible with the work of the Spirit guiding those who've begun to experience new-creation existence in which "the old has gone" (2 Cor. 5:17).

Some point out that our sin nature has not been obliterated in Christ, creating a possible scenario in which possession might occur. Yet a nature is a collection of attributes that describe a being; it does not compel that being to act. The continued presence of a sin nature does not compel Christians to act; the power of the Holy Spirit does, however, compel those in Christ toward actions that please God, including the ability to persist in salvation. So, while Christians cannot be possessed, 1 Peter 5:8 rightly warns about the spiritual warfare that is part of the Christian life. Being alert includes: (a) putting on God's armor, especially in the areas of meditating on Scripture and prayer (Eph. 6:11–18); (b) continually allowing the Holy Spirit to fill us (Eph. 5:18); and (c) paying close attention to our emotional life (Eph. 4:26–27; James 4:6–7).

Returning to the opening statement about horror movies as a form of Christian entertainment, it seems this should be a case-by-case choice. The genre should be analyzed just as any other form of entertainment should be. Such movies may remind us of the shared fallen experience, of our tendency to live in what philosopher Charles Taylor calls the "immanent frame," and may even open up discussions about the nature of evil.

7

THE DOCTRINE
OF HUMANITY AND SIN
(Anthropology and Hamartiology)

 **Image of God**

Humanity reflects God in form, relation, and rule—that is what it means to be created in His image (Lat. *imago Dei*) (Gen. 1:16–28). This image continues to be present in humanity even though it was corrupted by the Fall of Adam and Eve (Gen. 9:6; James 3:9). The lexical data of the two parallel words "image" (*tselem*) and "likeness" (*damuth*) given in Genesis 1:26 indicate the idea of form. The Septuagint's rendering of the Hebrew word *tselem* by the Greek word *eikōn* anticipates the common New Testament word for "image."

In short, humanity represents God in the same way a statue represents a false god. This may provide insight as to why God did not want graven images made of Him (Ex. 20:4)—He already had *living* statues to testify to His nature.

The term's connotations of form are also seen in the reference to Seth being in the "likeness" of Adam (Gen. 5:3). What this substantial representation consists of, though, is not self-evident in the biblical record. Yet we can deduce at least two areas included in this representation: mental capacities and moral capacities (Col. 3:10).

Genesis 1:27 defines the image of God with emphasis on the maleness and femaleness—that is, the relations—involved in what this image entails. This becomes clearer when the concept is repeated in Genesis 5:2. There, an added feature is seen when the male and female are collectively named "humankind" (*adam*). Hence, part of what it means to be made in God's image appears to be the capacity for relationships. One implication is that humanity's "personality" reflects the "personality" of God.

Strong images emerge out of the passage concerning humanity's subjugation of the created order on earth. The verbal expression "have dominion" (*radah*) in Genesis 1:26, 28 may indicate "to trample or stomp down" or "to master." The verbal expression "subdue" (*cabash*) is a slightly weaker term implying "to knead or tread." The implication for the image of God is that humanity has been given the authority to rule, and the substantial makeup to do so.

The traditional three ways for organizing the biblical material concerning the image of God—substantive, functional, and relational—all have some explanatory value. The *substantive* view sees the image as something within the makeup of humanity, a quality or characteristic that comprises their essence to some degree. This is the dominant view in church history. Animals do not possess the image of God; this suggests it is what makes us more like God and less like animals. The substantive view emphasizes the lexical forms of the words "image" and "likeness" (Gen. 1:26). Reason is the human faculty generally thought to be the human characteristic most associated with the image of God. A rational or moral component is the focus, since God is Spirit and does not have a body. Many who follow this approach suggest that the *imago Dei* consists of intellect, emotion, and will.

The *functional* view emphasizes activity. The divine image, then, is something humans do, not their substantive makeup. Usually in Scripture, human action involves stewarding, ruling, or exercising dominion over the earth and creation (Gen. 1:26, 28; Ps. 8:5–6).

Finally, the *relational* approach contends that the image is something humanity experiences in their response to both God and other humans (Gen. 1:27). Some seek to combine the three, usually nesting the functional and relational views as aspects of the substantive. Here the capacity to relate to God, like the Trinity relates to one another, or the capacity to rule, given as part of God's design, inform the full spectrum of human existence and activity.

Others understand the image of God Christologically. A strength of this approach is that Christ makes visible the invisible God (John 14:9). Paul describes Jesus as "the image of God" (2 Cor. 4:4) and "the Son" as the "image of the invisible God" (Col. 1:15). These verses suggest something more may be in view than the traditional approaches capture. In Ephesians 4:22–24, Paul contrasts the "old self" with the "new self, created to be like God." The same contrast occurs in Colossians 3:9–10, though this time he points out that "the new self . . . is being renewed in knowledge in the image of its Creator." The image is something received in Christ. The question is not what is the image of God but *who*—Jesus Christ. Learning to be human is a gift we receive through Christ by His resurrection (1 Cor. 15:21–22).

Why does this matter? It reminds us to see each other primarily as image-bearers of a holy God, and only secondarily through our particularity. This should discourage us from treating others like a commodity, which happens all too often in our culture. While ethnicity and race are important indicators of our identity and wonderful gifts from God, His image in us is what locates our value and worth. Racism, tribalism, and other ethnicity-based ideologies are sins, for they treat certain image-bearers as inferior to others (Acts 17:26; 1 Tim. 5:21; James 2:8–9). Relating to others as image-bearers can provide resources for reconciliation among groups that are and remain, as part of God's wonderful design, different.

25 Dichotomy and Trichotomy

Medical dramas on television—whether the old *St. Elsewhere*, the still-engaging *ER*, the over-the-top *House*, or the relationally oriented *Grey's Anatomy*—have always captured our attention. There are plenty of reasons for this, but one relates to the unknown elements of our own bodies and existence. But these shows also allow us to process ethical dilemmas and our view of life. Think about what happens once the diseased or massively injured person succumbs to their illness or injuries. The medical machines go quiet, the doctors or family members enact their roles as appropriate, while the deceased lies there lifeless. These shows allow us to consider the mysteries under our skin—theology does that as well, but with a little less drama. Are humans only bodies? Have the deceased gone out of existence? Is there more to them than what the medical machines measured? These are questions about our human nature—the way our material and immaterial aspects unite to form our essence or essential elements.

Theologians differ as to the essential elements of human nature. Some see the human person as trichotomous: made up of a body, soul, and spirit. Others contend humans are dichotomous: made up of a body and a soul. Still others argue for *monism*: humans are really only one element, and terms like "soul" or "spirit" are just ways to describe a person's physical life. The trichotomy view reaches back to Plato, whose categories influenced early theologians such as Origen and Clement of Alexandria. In the twentieth century, C. I. Scofield popularized this view among fundamentalists. Dichotomy, on the other hand, has been the dominant view of the church since Augustine. Reformed theologians rather uniformly accept this position.

Again, trichotomy is the belief that human nature consists of three elements: one material part (body) and two immaterial parts (soul and spirit). Traditionally, the soul is associated with the intellect, emotions, and will, while the spirit relates to God. Scriptural support for understanding human nature as body, soul, and spirit is found in 1 Thessalonians 5:23: "May God himself, the God of peace, sanctify you through and through. May your whole spirit, soul and body be kept blameless at the coming of our Lord Jesus Christ." Trichotomists see evidence here for two distinct parts of humanity in addition to the body: the "soul" (*psychē*), denoting humankind's immaterial aspect and which relates to their environment; and the "spirit" (*pneuma*), which relates to God. Others suggest this verse is not describing different immaterial aspects; rather, it is teaching God's desire for our complete sanctification. Trichotomists also point to Hebrews 4:12 as teaching a differentiation between soul and spirit: "For the word of God is alive and active. Sharper than any double-edged sword, it penetrates even to dividing soul and spirit, joints and marrow; it judges the thoughts and attitudes of the heart." Yet others simply see here the scriptural teaching that no element of the human person escapes the deep-searching work of God's Word.

Again, dichotomy describes the view that human nature has two essential parts, one material (physical body) and one immaterial (spiritual soul). Support for this view comes from the idea that "spirit" and "soul" are used interchangeably in Scripture. In John 12:27, Jesus speaks of His *soul* being troubled, but in John 13:21, it is His *spirit* that is troubled. Yet no distinction of experience is indicated in the context. "Body and soul" or "body and spirit" constitute the totality of human nature. Further scriptural support for this comes from Matthew 10:28: "Do not be afraid of those who kill the body but cannot kill the soul. Rather, be afraid of the One who can destroy both soul and body in hell." This passage is difficult to understand, unless "soul" and "spirit" are synonyms. Paul uses "spirit" similarly: "For my part, even though I am not physically present, I am with you in spirit. As one who is present with you in this way, I have already passed judgment in the name of our Lord Jesus on the one who has been doing this" (1 Cor. 5:3). Paul points to his spirit as that aspect of his nature addressing the problem in Corinth. He continues in 5:5: "Hand this man over to Satan for the destruction of the flesh, so that his spirit may be saved on the day of the Lord." When this verse is compared with Matthew 10:28, it is likely "soul" and "spirit" are interchangeable terms.

Both trichotomy and dichotomy are "dualistic" positions at odds with materialistic *monism*, a view that accounts for the immaterial part of human nature by appealing to neurobiological processes. What trichotomous and dichotomous theologians, as dualists, ascribe to the soul or spirit, monists connect to activity in the brain and the central nervous system. Obviously, monism destabilizes the traditional view of the existence of the soul, along with theological conclusions related to consciousness and morality. Additionally, the monist position is incompatible with the intermediate state, since the human person ceases to exist once the body with its neurological processes stop at death. The dualist position accounts for the disembodied, intermediate state (2 Cor. 5:1–9).

So, the next time you are watching your favorite medical drama, and those machines go quiet, remember there is more to a human person than what those machines can measure. In addition, while theologians differ over the way to describe our immaterial aspect, we can be confident, with the apostle Paul, that "to be absent from the body" for those in Christ means to be "at home with the Lord" (2 Cor. 5:8 NASB).

26 ❯ Traducianism and Creationism

Where did our soul originate? This sounds like a question one asks when they can't sleep after a long day of binge-watching a science-fiction series on Netflix. However, it is much more than that. Movies, television shows, and novels offer their own vision of the nature and origination of the soul, or, as in the 2018 movie *Replicas*, scoff at its existence and present a materialist vision in which humans are reduced to computer code. The Christian theological vision of the human person is important to clarify in our contemporary moment.

Traducianism is the view that both a person's soul and body are received or transmitted as part of natural, physical processes from their parents. Tertullian (ca. 155–240) was an early proponent of this view. He developed it in response to the teaching of the *pre-existence of the soul* evident among some Gnostics, an early heretical group that opposed several areas of orthodox teaching. Tertullian's position is that, at the moment of conception, the body and soul of the person are determined (*A Treatise on the Soul*, 3:1). Scriptural support for this position relies on a claim that humans are created in God's image and have the ability to produce children with a body and soul. Other creatures can reproduce "according to their kind," so the same idea would apply to humans (Gen. 1:24, 27).

Some would respond that a child in their "likeness" and "image" might indicate Seth inherited his soul from Adam and Eve (Gen. 5:3); it could also indicate God created a soul for Seth in line with key indexes of identity consistent with his parents. Others point to Hebrews 7:10, since it teaches that when Melchizedek met Abraham, "Levi was still in the body of his ancestor." The suggestion is that physical processes are the means through which identity is transmitted. Others would note, however, that this should not be understood literally, for Levi's genetic material would not have been discernible at that point. Traducianism removes God's agency, some argue, in directly creating a sinful soul. Nevertheless, God causes other events to occur in the world that do not directly implicate Him. The similarities in relation to sin among a kinship group would be accounted for via the normal socialization processes (Ex. 20:5).

Creationism is the view that God creates a new soul for each person that, at some point, is united with the person's sinful body that came from their parents. Jerome (ca. 347–419) was an early proponent of this view, though his broader concern lay with debates over the pre-existence of the soul and original sin, some of which occurred in a letter from Augustine (*Letter* 166). Supporters of this view contend there is ample evidence in Scripture that God is the one who creates our spiritual soul (e.g., Isa. 42:5; Zech. 12:1; Heb. 12:9). Others counter that this makes God the direct author of sin or moral evil, in relation to humanity.

Creationism maintains the original creation account, which distinguishes the creation of the body from the dirt and the soul as a direct result of God's breath (Gen. 2:7), a perspective maintained throughout Scripture (Num. 16:22; Eccl. 12:7; Heb. 12:9). Others argue that Genesis 2:2 teaches God has already ceased His creative work, and thus these verses are not as probative as they first appear (but see John 5:17). Psalm 127:3 declares: "Children are a heritage from the LORD, offspring a reward from him." This seems to suggest that God is active at some level in the process. Creationism relies on the concept of secondary causes to explain the way He accomplishes His creative purposes in the world. This allows for some degree of parental agency in the soul-creation process, though the degree or manner in which this occurs is not stated explicitly in Scripture.

Traducianism and creationism developed as theological

positions in response to several debates, including whether souls pre-exist. The pre-existence of the soul developed originally in Platonism, a philosophical system that was popular as Christianity emerged, causing theologians and pastors to engage it in defense against false teaching. The Platonic system held that the immortal soul emanates from its heavenly state and joins temporarily with a body; after its transitory existence on earth, it returns to its abode in the heavens—only to begin the cycle again. A Christianized version of the pre-existence of the soul emerged with an early theologian named Origen (ca. 184–253). This version contends that a human soul existed in heaven with God, and that as a human is conceived, God joins one of these pre-existent souls—which is tainted by sin—with the developing body in the womb. Origen's views were eventually condemned at the Second Council of Constantinople in AD 553. What Origen, Tertullian, Jerome, and Augustine were trying to understand was the idea of original sin.

The answers these early theologians gave in regard to original sin hinged on their view on the origin of the soul. This reminds us of why getting the various aspects of our theology clear is important more broadly. Specifically with regard to the soul, our culture wrestles with this question all the time. Gabriel Squailia's novel *Dead Boys* grapples with the nature of the soul, and Robert J. Sawyer's *The Terminal Experiment* tries to determine whether there is empirical evidence for the soul and the nature of human consciousness. While these novels offer little in the way of truth, they serve as reminders for the types of questions our culture wonders about—and the opportunity we have to share with them God's truth about the nature, origin, and the destination of the body-soul unity.

27 › Sin

No one wants to talk about sin—unless it's to highlight those culturally defined "sins" *others* commit, while curiously overlooking their own. Some downplay the sinfulness of sin by using it as a title for their scrumptious chocolate pie or lampooning its existence in movies, books, or music. Others think only of the seven deadly sins—pride, envy, sloth, greed, wrath, lust, and gluttony—which have a theological basis going back to Bonaventure (1221–1274). But are they a sufficient definition? No, although the seven deadly sins are helpful shorthand reminders for some of the ways Satan seeks to move Christians toward setting their affections on this world rather than God (1 John 2:16; see **Satan**).

Sin is any act against or lack regarding God's moral law (1 John 3:4; Rom. 4:15; James 4:17). It is unrighteousness or unbelief (1 John 5:17; Rom. 14:23) that results in our guilt before God (Ps. 130:3), for it goes against His character and will (Gen. 39:9; Ps. 51:4). In theology, sin is not a stand-alone concept; it is connected to the fall of Adam and the degree to which humanity is implicated in that fall (Rom. 5:12; Gen. 2:16–17; 3:1–24; see **Original Sin**). The Hebrew word *chata'*, which in context may signify "missing the mark," functions metaphorically to describe sin as missing the standard of God's moral law (Ex. 32:30–33; Josh. 7:20). In the Greek New Testament, *hamartia* serves as the dominant word for sin; it maintains much of the idea of "missing the mark" in relation to God's standard (Rom. 5:12; 6:23; 1 John 1:8). Another Hebrew word, *'awal*, often translated in English Bibles as "iniquity" or "injustice," provides a social description of what departing from God's course entails (Lev. 19:15; Ps. 53:1). The social ideas of "iniquity" and "injustice" are picked up in the use of the Greek word *anomia*, highlighting also ideas of "lawlessness" (Matt. 24:12; Rom. 4:7; 1 John 3:4). These terms bring to the fore the relevance of actions or deeds in identifying sins.

Sin might include transgressing explicit or implicit laws prohibited on the basis of God's holy character. It may also involve a failure to engage in something virtuous as revealed in God's moral law. As Paul wrote in Romans 3:23, "For all have sinned and fall short of the glory of God." Theologically, to "fall short of the glory of God" is a broad conceptual framework for understanding sin as acts that were done but should not have been, or ones that should have been but were not. Theologians describe these, respectively, as sins of commission and sins of omission (James 4:17). The *moral law*, sometimes described as the *natural law*, includes the rules for human conduct discernible from God's created world. Evangelicals are sometimes hesitant to incorporate this into their theology, but it serves as an important part of Catholic theology. The moral law is also used to describe one of the threefold divisions of the Mosaic Law among theologians, the other two being the civil and ceremonial. The claim is that these latter two are no longer binding on Christians, while the moral law is since it contains transcendent principles that express God's character. In the Reformed tradition, the Ten Commandments are seen as those moral instructions that provide normative guidance for humanity; some include the Lord's Prayer and the Creeds in this as further normative guidance for the church. Others only focus on the gospel and the commands found in the New Testament; the Old Testament is merely directives for Israel, with possible applications for Christians discerned through a process of locating principles for us to live by today.

Theologians have long attempted to uncover the essence of sin, and pride is generally seen as the core. Selfishness may be even more central, for Paul begins his vice list by stating, "People will be lovers of themselves" (2 Tim. 3:2), and he makes it clear that in light of Jesus' death on the cross we should no longer live for ourselves but for Christ (2 Cor. 5:15). This suggests that sin is the elevation of the self and the demotion of God. The work of the Spirit in the new creation reverses the processes of selfishness that reveal themselves in various "deeds of the flesh" (Gal. 5:22–23; Eph. 5:18–21). These aberrant patterns of embodiment point to the idea that sin also has a cognitive component—unbelief.

Many of these ideas come together in John 16:7–11. In verse 7, Jesus highlights the work of the Spirit as a continuation of His ministry. In verse 8, part of the Spirit's work is to make explicit the world's cognitive deficiencies when it comes to "sin and righteousness and judgment." In verse 9, Jesus brings to the fore the crucial condition that produces sin: it is "because people do not believe in me." In verse 10, the "righteous" standard associated with God's character is evident. People sin when they do not conform to God's standard for righteousness (Gk. *adikeō*; Rom. 1:18; Col. 3:25; Heb. 8:12). In verse 11, both the idea of "judgment" and the statement about "the prince of this world" remind us that our struggles with sin are part of a larger cosmic battle (see **Satan**). This is especially important to remember when seeking to live in the context of global pathologies and structural inequalities, as well as long-standing struggles with addictions and victimizations on the personal level.

Why does this matter? A theologically sound understanding of sin will help us have more realistic expectations when we encounter other people. And it can help reduce our personal discouragement with our own behaviors and struggles. Understanding sin as the core foundational problem for humanity also better informs our practice in ministry. If we do not think the gospel is the ultimate solution to the world's sin problem, it is unlikely that gospel proclamation will maintain its place in the primary mission of the church (see **The Church**).

28 > Original Sin

The blame game—it's one of our favorites to play. Why take responsibility when something goes wrong; it's much easier (not to mention more enjoyable) to lay the fault at the feet of another, right? *Fast-food restaurants are to blame for my weight issues. My pastor's poor preaching inhibits my spiritual growth.* This is nothing new: Adam blamed Eve (Gen. 3:12), and Aaron, after producing a golden calf, blamed the Israelites for his idolatry (Ex. 32:22–24). So, whom do we blame for our sinful actions? Paul blames Adam (Rom. 5:12), but how are we to understand this?

Original sin is the idea that all of humanity enters the world alienated from God and is thus culpable before Him as corrupt and guilty. This state derives from Adam's fall in the garden of Eden in Genesis 3, and it results in humanity being born with a *sin nature* (Ps. 51:5). This nature—a collection of attributes that make up a being—means that humans have no capacity to do anything that commends them to God. Several results come from original sin. We are born guilty before God, leading to divine disfavor (Matt. 7:4–5; 12:34; 1 John 1:8). If left in that condition, we would eventually experience His justice (Rom. 12:19; Heb. 10:30). Physical death became part of the human experience (Gen. 3:19, 22; Rom. 5:12). Also, various personal and social effects developed from original sin. On a personal level: (a) enslavement to sin (Rom. 7:14); (b) relational distance (Gen. 3:11–12); (c) self-deception (Jer. 17:9); and (d) cognitive deficiencies in regard to our conscience (1 Tim. 4:2). On a social level: (a) racism or tribalism (Acts 17:26); (b) economic inequality (2 Cor. 8:13–15); and (c) other identity-based conflicts (Gal. 2:11–14).

There are several views concerning original sin, all trying to make sense of Paul's statement in Romans 5:12: "Therefore, just as sin entered the world through one man, and death through sin, and in this way death came to all people, because all sinned." Augustine (354–430) claimed that humanity really participated in Adam's sin. This is often called the *realist* position, since Adam's posterity were in some way present in him when he fell (*The City of God*, 2:251). Just as Levi paid tithes to Melchizedek by being present in the body of Abraham (Heb. 7:9–10), so corruption and guilt were imputed via the "loins" to all of humanity as Adam's progeny.

Pelagius (354–418) maintained that God directly created each soul innocent, not guilty of Adam's sin (see **Traducianism** and **Creationism**). Pelagius simply thought Adam was a poor example. In his reading, Romans 5:12 does not affect humanity in general; only the acts of sin people themselves commit are imputed to them. Humanity did not die because of original sin, but because of the law of nature. Pelagius also thought each person possessed a perfect free will, in contrast to the bondage of the will evident in Augustine. Pelagius did think people will experience a personal fall, though he left open the possibility that a person could choose to live a life without sin. His views were condemned at the Council of Carthage in AD 418 but have continued on throughout church history. A later development of this view, semi-Pelagianism, was condemned at the Council of Orange in AD 529.

Jacobus Arminius (1560–1609) rejected the idea that humanity was guilty because of Adam's sin, but he acknowledged humanity had a corruptive influence. In his view, when people purposefully choose to sin, even though they could choose differently, God imputes or reckons sin to them and declares them guilty. Humanity does not possess original righteousness due to Adam's sin; this distinguishes Arminianism from Pelagianism. Arminius's innovation is that God confers on humans a distinctive work of the Holy Spirit that can neutralize the effect of inherited depravity. This makes obedience possible on the condition that the human will cooperates with the Holy Spirit (see **Conversion**). Total depravity is rejected in this view; Romans 5:12 is imputed to humans only once they sin themselves.

Johannes Cocceius (1603–1669) developed the standard *Reformed* view. Adam was humanity's federal head, and God entered into a covenant of works whereby Adam would be blessed if he obeyed. The result of his failure, however, was that all of humanity fell into evil and death. The depravity of humanity was total; sin and all of its guilt were imputed to humanity because of Adam's sin and his federal union with us. Paul's comparison between Adam and Christ favors the federal view over the realism of Pelagianism. However, many find the idea of inherited guilt offensive. This is nothing new; the Israelites struggled with the same idea. There was, however, an awareness that their ancestors were sinful; nevertheless, blame could not finally be shifted (Ezek. 18:24; Jer. 16:11–13). Even though many struggle with the idea of Adam serving as our representative, our lack of conformity to God's law suggests his sin is more evident in us than we care to admit.

Total depravity indicates that every aspect of the human person is infected with sin (Jer. 17:9; Rom. 7:18), while total inability highlights the idea that humanity can do nothing on its own to reorient itself toward God and away from the sinful self (Rom. 8:8–10). Sin affects the entire person, not just one aspect (Eph. 2:1–3). This is not to say that unregenerate humanity doesn't do anything that might be deemed virtuous—it clearly does (Matt. 7:11). The claim here is that unregenerate humanity does nothing that would enable them to change their condition in regard to their sinful nature (Rom. 6:6; Eph. 2:12).

Why does this doctrine matter? Often original sin and total depravity are misunderstood, and it's important to ask questions concerning what is actually meant by words when they're used. Total depravity is a load-bearing distinction between Calvinism and Arminianism. As followers of Christ, we can be reminded of who we are now. Once we were spiritually dead but now we are spiritually alive (Eph. 2:1–5), by the regenerating work of the Holy Spirit (John 3:1–8). While the reign of sin has been broken, we, by the ongoing work of the Spirit, still need to be vigilant: "Put to death, therefore, whatever belongs to your earthly nature" (Col. 3:5). A good understanding of this doctrine helps us to be empathic with others struggling with sin, all while maintaining the clear message of the gospel (2 Cor. 4:2–6; Eph. 2:9). Finally, it motivates our worship as we remember all that God has done for us by grace (Rom. 7:24–25; Eph. 3:20–21).

8

THE DOCTRINE OF SALVATION
(Soteriology)

 **Salvation**

Suppose on a beautiful summer afternoon you wade into a waist-high pool to enjoy a cool swim. Suddenly the lifeguard splashes into the water after you, grabs you, and starts to drag you back to the side. When you indignantly resist, he tells you to stop fighting his efforts to save you from drowning. Most likely you would consider this lifeguard to be delusional. Why? Because you are not drowning in the first place, so you do not need saving. The very idea of salvation presupposes something destructive from which you need rescue.

In the previous chapter, we saw that fallen human beings have a fundamental problem: sin. Its presence is everywhere, its terrible effects incalculable. It enslaves and victimizes human beings even as they willingly perpetrate it. Worse still, it leaves us completely alienated from God and subject to His just and fearful wrath. To top it all off, there is nothing we can do to deliver ourselves from it. This is what makes the gospel genuinely good news, for it declares salvation in Christ Jesus. Salvation is deliverance from sin in all its forms and effects through Jesus Christ.

Just think of how comprehensive this deliverance is. If sin brings God's just penalty of death, salvation delivers us from God's just wrath and declares us righteous in His sight (Gal. 3:13; Rom. 1:18–3:31; 5:12–21). If sin holds us in bondage, salvation breaks its chains and frees us to serve Christ (Rom. 6:1–7, 19–22). If sin corrupts everything we are and do, salvation transforms us into Christ's perfect image (1 John 3:2–3; Rom. 8:29; 6:13). If sin distorts and defiles the world around us (Rom. 3:17–19; Eccl. 1:2; Rom. 8:18–25), salvation culminates in the perfection of the new heaven and new earth (Rev. 21–22).

God's agenda in salvation is grand indeed, but it comes in stages. Sometimes believers think of their salvation only in the past tense, in that they are *already* saved. This is certainly true, but God is not finished with believers once they trust Christ. As we just saw, His agenda is more than delivering us from hell, as great as that may be. For a believer, then, salvation is a past, present, and future reality (Titus 2:11–14; 1 Peter 1:3–9). The gospel is not "old news" once a person trusts in Christ. It is good news for our present and future as well as our past.

Most religions claim to save people, whether from sin or something else. And in virtually all of them, human beings work to achieve their own salvation. The salvation proclaimed in the gospel is radically different. The theology of the Protestant Reformation nicely summarized this message in the *five solas* (the term *sola* is Latin for "alone"): We are saved by grace alone (*sola gratia*), through faith alone (*sola fide*), in Christ alone (*solus Christus*), to the glory of God alone (*soli Deo gloria*), according to Scripture alone (*sola scriptura*). We have already discussed Scripture alone (*sola scriptura*) in connection with Scripture's authority (see **The Characteristics of Scripture**); in this context it is a reminder that the message of salvation is rooted in the final authority of Scripture. But let's focus more on the other terms here.

We are saved by *grace alone. Grace* is God's unmerited favor granted kindly to His sinful creatures. In many ways all human beings receive God's grace in, for example, the blessings of life (Acts 17:25), sustenance (Acts 14:17), basic morality (Rom. 2:14–15), and governmental order (Rom. 13:1–7). This is called *common grace*. But everyone who is saved has received a special kind of grace beyond common grace. This *saving grace*, as the name indicates, is the grace by which God grants salvation in all its fullness to His people. And it is solely due to this grace that we are saved (Eph. 2:1–10). In no way do we earn our salvation; indeed, we contribute nothing to it. Our salvation is not our own doing but the gift of God (Eph. 2:8).

This is where faith comes in. Our salvation is God's gracious gift received *through faith alone*. Faith is contrasted with works, which refer to the human effort to earn God's favor by doing good deeds. If salvation were a result of my good works, I could then boast. I could take pride in what I did to earn my salvation. In contrast, faith is only God-centered. It acknowledges our inability to save ourselves and instead trusts God to save us in loving mercy, despite our unworthiness (Eph. 2:8–9). Through faith we receive God's gift of salvation and trust Him completely for it.

But faith is not an empty vessel. We are not saved merely by having faith in something; we are saved by the object of our faith, the One we are trusting for salvation. In short, we are saved solely through faith *in Christ alone*. Our salvation is entirely the work of God in Christ (1 Cor. 1:26–31; 1 Tim. 2:3–7). It is realized only in who Christ is and what He has done. This is why our union with Christ through faith is the heart of our salvation (see **Union with Christ**). It is also why we don't need additional mediators (clergy or saints) or our own good works to supplement Christ's perfect work (Heb. 7:23–25; 9:11–28).

Further, salvation in Christ alone means that it cannot be found apart from Christ. This is called *religious exclusivism*, which maintains that since salvation can only be found through faith in Christ, no other religion can save. This contrasts with two other notions common in our day. *Religious pluralism* maintains that salvation can be found in many religions because there are many ways to God. But this view contradicts the Bible's insistence that salvation is found exclusively in Christ (Acts 4:12; John 14:6; 1 John 5:12). *Religious inclusivism* agrees that salvation does indeed come only through

Christ, but it argues that people do not need to trust specifically in Christ for salvation if they have not heard the gospel. This view, however, does not deal adequately with the Bible's teaching about the centrality of gospel proclamation and faith specifically in Christ (Rom. 10:8–17; John 3:18).

If salvation is by grace alone through faith alone in Christ alone, then it is also *to the glory of God alone*. God gets all the credit for our salvation. Having contributed nothing to our salvation, we have nothing to boast about in ourselves (Rom. 4:1–8). All our praise, honor, and worship must instead be directed to God alone for our salvation (1 Cor. 1:26–31; Rom. 11:33–36). "Let the one who boasts, boast in the Lord" (1 Cor. 1:31). What the Lord has done for us in Christ deserves a much closer look. That's what we will be doing in this chapter.

30 ▶ Election

If salvation depends exclusively on God, why isn't everyone saved? After all, God wants everyone to be saved, doesn't He (1 Tim. 2:4)? Perhaps God simply makes salvation available to everyone, and then each person chooses whether to cooperate with His saving grace (and be saved) or resist it (and be lost). Or perhaps the decision about whom to save is God's alone, not dependent in any way on human choice. This is where the doctrine of *predestination* comes in. Predestination is God's decision from eternity past about who will be saved and who will not. As the definition implies, there are two sides of predestination. On the positive side is election, God's choice of who will be saved. On the negative side is *reprobation*, God's choice of those who will not be saved. Because election is central to the debate, we will focus there.

Among evangelicals, there are three primary views on the doctrine of election. The first view is *unconditional election*. This view maintains that in eternity past God chose to save some human beings based solely on His sovereign will. It is unconditional because His choice is not based on any condition people meet, whether what they do or who they are. Advocates point to passages like Ephesians 1:3–14, which declares that God, "who works all things according to the counsel of his will" (v. 11 ESV), chose us in Christ "before the foundation of the world" (v. 4) and "according to the purpose of his will" (v. 5 ESV). Similarly, 2 Timothy 1:9 declares that God "saved us and called us to a holy calling, not because of our works but because of his own purpose and grace, which he gave us in Christ Jesus before the ages began" (ESV). And Paul's teaching in Romans 8:29–30, expanded in 9:6–29, testifies powerfully to God's unconditional choice of the redeemed (see also John 6:36–37, 44; 15:6; 2 Thess. 2:13).

Unconditional election is Calvinistic (see **Calvinism**); the remaining two views are decidedly not. *Conditional election* affirms that God chooses individuals in eternity past because He foresees that they will freely believe in Christ. Advocates of this view maintain that it preserves a robust human freedom and puts responsibility for accepting or rejecting the gospel squarely on the shoulders of each person. They also appeal to 1 Peter 1:1–2, which says that God's elect are chosen "according to the foreknowledge of God," and Romans 8:29–30, which declares that "those God foreknew he also predestined to be conformed to the image of his Son."

These two texts raise a related debate about the nature of *foreknowledge*. Scholars agree that foreknowledge in the New Testament can refer to advanced knowledge either of facts (factual knowledge) or of people (relational knowledge). The question is, which sense of foreknowledge is in view in 1 Peter 1 and Romans 8? Advocates of conditional election insist that these texts speak of advanced knowledge of *facts*. God knows in eternity past who will freely choose Him and, based on that knowledge, He chooses them. Calvinists, on the other hand, argue that these texts speak of advanced knowledge of *people* (relational knowledge). God determines to enter into relationship with some people in eternity past (the elect), and then at the proper time grants His saving grace to them so that they can and will believe. Put differently, if conditional election says that God chose us because we will choose Him, unconditional election says that we will choose to believe in Him because God first chose us.

The third view, *corporate election*, bypasses the focus of the first two views because it insists that God does not choose particular persons at all. Instead, it maintains that God chose to save the body of believers—the church—as a group. But He does not choose the particular persons who decide to become part of that body by faith; that is their choice. Like conditional election, then, this view also is not Calvinistic. To be sure, all three views would agree that there is a corporate element to election, but the unconditional and conditional views insist that the group and the individuals making up that group cannot be so easily separated. After all, God does save each believer individually (see Rom. 8:28–30), and so each believer's name is written in the book of life (Rev. 3:5; 21:27; cf. 13:8; 17:8; 20:12, 15).

What about the other side of predestination, the doctrine of reprobation? To be sure, the Bible does speak of this doctrine (Rom. 9:14–22; 11:7–10; 1 Peter 2:7–8; Jude 4). Advocates of conditional and corporate election, however, do not stress reprobation since they maintain that the choice and responsibility for unbelievers' condemnation rests solely with them. Advocates of unconditional election (Calvinists), in contrast, teach both election and reprobation, but they typically insist the two are not symmetrical. That is, God chooses to save His elect and to pass over the non-elect. Because all human beings are sinful and do not want God, the non-elect will inevitably reject the Lord and face His just condemnation.

Besides creating controversy, what are the practical effects of the doctrine of election? In Scripture, this doctrine is clearly meant to encourage believers that they belong to Christ and that He will finish His good work in them (e.g.,

Rom. 8:28–39). Further, it actually functions as a spur to evangelism, for the evangelist can be confident that God has elect who have yet to come to Him through the preaching of the gospel (2 Tim. 2:10). Above all else, election is a cause of praise to the Lord who has chosen to save us even when we would never have chosen Him if left to ourselves (Eph. 1:3–14); solely because of God's saving grace, the elect will inevitably turn to the Lord in conversion.

31 > Conversion

If you ask most evangelical Christians to give their testimony, they will tell you the story of how they became followers of Christ. We typically identify this beginning of our Christian lives with the time of our conversion. At our conversion we willingly turn from our sin in repentance and turn to Christ in faith, resulting in our salvation. Conversion thus involves two elements, flip sides of the same coin: repentance and faith.

Repentance is our willing turn away from sin (Ps. 51; Luke 18:9–14; 2 Cor. 7:8–11). Theologians often point out that repentance has three aspects. Intellectually, our view of sin changes and we see more clearly what it is really like, how destructive it is to us, and how heinous it is in the sight of the living God. If I see sin for what it really is, it naturally follows that there will be an emotional response. I will come to hate my sin, feel sorrow for its presence and effects in my life, and want deliverance from it. This in turn is accompanied by a volitional element. I purpose to set my life in a new direction away from sin. In short, to be saved from sin, one must actually *want* to be saved from sin.

But saving repentance is not merely turning over a new leaf when I feel badly about my wrongdoing. Many people seek to do that; just think of our annual New Year's resolutions. Indeed, such an endeavor is at the heart of human religion's attempt to earn salvation. In contrast, saving repentance is inextricably bound to saving faith in Christ (Mark 1:15; Acts 20:21). For when we truly repent, our sin prompts us to turn from that sin in hope and trust to the only One who can truly deal with our problem.

Saving *faith* is believing and trusting in Jesus Christ for deliverance from our sin and eternal reconciliation with God (John 3:14–18; 6:35–40; Acts 13:38–39; Rom. 10:8–17). As with repentance, saving faith has three aspects. It begins with knowledge of the gospel message about Christ; one must understand who Christ is and what He has done to save us. In addition, one must believe that the gospel message about Christ is actually true. Still, knowing and believing about Christ is not enough. One must also trust oneself entirely to Christ for salvation. Consider a chair, for example. I can recognize a chair and understand that it is designed to hold me up if I sat in it. I can also believe that it would hold me up were I to sit in it. But the chair avails me nothing until I actually entrust myself to it and sit in it. Similarly, anyone who comes to Christ for salvation rests in Him alone for salvation.

But how is conversion even possible? If fallen human beings left to themselves are dead in trespasses and sins (Eph. 2:1), hostile to God, and unable to submit to His law (Rom. 8:7), how can they turn to Christ in faith? At this point, it might be helpful first to discuss how Calvinists answer these questions. Calvinists insist that our conversion is *monergistic*, that is, it is due solely to the gracious work of God in us. God does His work in us through the *gospel call*, the sharing of the good news of Jesus Christ through God's people (Rom. 10:8–17). But along with proclamation of the gospel comes *effective calling*—God's internal, special work of grace in the heart of God's elect ensuring that they will respond positively to the gospel call (Rom. 8:30; 1 Cor. 1:22–31; John 6:37, 44, 64–65; Acts 16:13–15). Accompanying effective calling is *regeneration*. In regeneration, the Holy Spirit imparts spiritual life to those who are spiritually dead so that they are "born again" to a new life of faith in Christ (John 3:1–8; 1 Peter 1:22–23; Eph. 2:4–5). Having been internally changed with a new heart and new affections, they necessarily and willingly turn from sin to Christ and are saved (1 John 5:1).

Non-Calvinists reject the Calvinist account of how fallen people can turn to Christ. Some maintain that sinful, fallen human beings still have the capacity in some small way to respond to the offer of salvation. More commonly, however, non-Calvinists agree that fallen human beings are unable on their own to respond to the gospel. But they deny that effective calling exists and that regeneration precedes conversion. Instead, they believe that God imparts to all human beings (or at least to all who hear the gospel) a *prevenient grace* that restores to them the ability to choose either to accept saving grace or to resist it. In short, they hold to *synergism*, the belief that conversion can only happen if the human being cooperates with God's saving grace instead of resisting it. Regeneration then follows conversion, rather than being the basis for conversion, as it is in Calvinism.

Whether monergistic or synergistic, conversion results in radical change in the lives of new believers, for when they turn from sin to Christ in faith, they are saved. The next several terms describe in more detail the blessings that salvation brings.

32 ▶ Union with Christ

We all like receiving gifts, whether at birthdays, Christmas, or some other time. When people give us a gift, we thank them and think fondly of them from time to time as we enjoy it. But once we receive the gift from them, we can enjoy it apart from them. Salvation too is a gift—the gift of God (Eph. 2:8)—but it is not like Christmas or birthday presents that can be enjoyed apart from the giver. Salvation is inherently personal, a gift inseparable from the one who secured it and gives it. Christ Himself is our salvation. When we trust Him at conversion, we are joined with Him, and in Him we receive all the blessings of salvation. This is called union with Christ. Paul summarizes it nicely in Ephesians 1:3 when he says that God the Father "has blessed us *in Christ* with every spiritual blessing" (ESV, emphasis added). There is no salvation apart from the Savior.

Consider some of the ways Scripture pictures our intimate union with Christ. Frequently Scripture says that believers are in Christ (e.g., 1 Cor. 1:30; 2 Cor. 5:17, 21; Phil. 3:8–9) and that Christ is in believers (e.g., 2 Cor. 13:5; Col. 1:27; Eph. 3:17). Christ is pictured as the living vine who gives life and sustenance to believers as branches (John 15:1–11). Christ is also pictured as the head of the body, and believers are all parts of that body in organic union with one another in Him (Eph. 1:22–23; 4:14–16; 5:23; Col. 1:17–18; cf. Rom. 12:4–5; 1 Cor. 12:12–13). Perhaps even more powerfully, Scripture uses marriage to present the personal, intimate relationship between Christ and believers (Eph. 5:22–33; 1 Cor. 11:3; Rev. 19:7; 21:9).

What is this union like? It is life-giving, for our very spiritual life and growth comes only in our relationship to Christ. Christ is our life (Col. 3:4; John 11:25–26; Gal. 2:20). In addition, it is intimate, personally relating us to Christ in a way that touches every part of our being and shapes our identity. Further, the union is Trinitarian. That is, in Christ we are brought into intimate relationship with the Father and the Spirit. Our union with Christ brings union with the Father (John 17:2–23; 1 John 4:15; 1 Thess. 1:1). And not only does the Spirit unite us with Christ and mediate His presence in us (1 Cor. 12:13; Rom. 8:9–11), but Christ also is the one through whom we receive the Spirit (John 14:26; Matt. 3:11; Luke 24:49; Acts 1:5; 2:33; Eph. 1:13). Our union with Christ is also judicial, in that our standing before God as judge is legally inseparable from Jesus Christ (see **Justification**). Finally, this union is corporate, for in being united with Christ believers are also organically united with one another as the body of Christ (Eph. 4:15–16).

This amazing union means that what is true of Him is applied to me. The good news of what He has done becomes my story. In Him, I am joined to the new redeemed humanity out of the old fallen humanity in Adam (Rom. 5:12–20). In Him, His perfect life and righteousness become mine, sinner though I am (1 Cor. 1:30; Rom. 5:18–19; Phil. 3:9). In Him, my sin which He bore is paid in full (Rom. 3:23–26; 2 Cor. 5:21; 1 Peter 2:24). In Him, I died to what I was in Adam and am raised to new life, a life that changes me and secures my final resurrection (Rom. 6:1–23; Eph. 2:4–6). And as He is now exalted at the right hand of the Father, so now in Him I am spiritually seated with Him in heavenly places with future, eternal glory guaranteed (Eph. 2:4–6; 1:19–23; Col. 3:3–4). In Him, as I live this life to His glory, He is in me and with me and working through me to make me more like Him and fulfill His calling for me (Matt. 28:20; John 15:5; 1 Cor. 15:58; Phil. 1:21; 4:13).

Consider just one facet of our union with Christ. In Christ each of us is *adopted* as God's child (Gal. 3:26; Eph. 1:4–5). He is the beloved Son in whom the Father is well-pleased (Matt. 3:17), and in Him we participate in His sonship by faith (John 1:12–13; 1 John 3:1–3; 5:1). This reality represents a remarkable *reconciliation* with God, for prior to being joined to Christ we were enemies of God (Rom. 5:10) and "children of wrath" (Eph. 2:3). Because of our adoption in Christ, we are also reconciled with one another and become brothers and sisters in Christ (Eph. 2:11–22). Because of our adoption in Christ, we are joint heirs with Him (Rom. 8:16–17). Because of our adoption in Christ, we can boldly approach the throne of our Father in prayer (Eph. 2:18; 3:11–12; Heb. 4:16; Rom. 5:1–2). Because of our adoption in Christ, we experience blessings that come from being children of our heavenly Father, including His loving care (Matt. 6:25–34) and discipline (Heb. 12:5–11).

There are many other facets of our union with Christ beyond our adoption and reconciliation. By virtue of our union with Christ, we are regenerated (Eph. 2:5, 10), justified (Rom. 3:21–26; Phil. 3:9), sanctified (1 Cor. 1:30; John 15:4–5; Eph. 4:15–16), secured (Rom. 8:31–39; John 10:27–28), and will be resurrected (1 Cor. 15:20–22; Rom. 6:5) to glory (Rom. 8:29–30; 1 John 3:2). In a sense, we were in Christ even before we were saved. For the Father "chose us in him before the foundation of the world" (Eph. 1:3–4 ESV), guaranteeing that in the future, we would be united with Christ by faith to experience the blessings of salvation. In sum, to talk of union with Christ is to talk about our salvation in all its facets, for all the blessings of salvation flow out of it. Let's consider more closely these blessings of salvation in Christ.

33 Justification

Do you ever feel guilty—*really guilty*—for something you have done? Almost everyone does, and for good reason. These feelings are mere glimpses of our status before the living, holy God. Written over everything we are and do is the verdict "guilty," and there is nothing we can do on our own to change that (Rom. 3:19–20). Humans long to be freed from such guilt, to experience what David proclaimed: "Blessed is the one whose transgression is forgiven, whose sin is covered. Blessed is the man against whom the Lord counts no iniquity" (Ps. 32:1–2a ESV).

David's exultation is no pipe dream. After meticulously laying out His case in Romans 1:18–3:20 that all human beings without exception are sinners guilty before God and helpless to save themselves, the apostle Paul boldly restores hope in the next verse: "But now the righteousness of God has been manifested apart from the law" (Rom. 3:21a ESV). This hope comes through Christ's work of redemption, received by faith and justifying us before the holy God (Rom. 3:21b–26). Justification is God's legal judgment that all believers' sins are forgiven and that they are righteous in His sight, based on the redemptive work of Christ received by faith.

Let's unpack this marvelous doctrine of justification a little more by looking at five of its characteristics. First, justification is forensic, a legal verdict from God (Rom. 3:19–28; 4:4–5; 5:1; 8:1–2, 33–34). It is God's judicial declaration regarding our legal status that we are righteous rather than condemned in His sight. It is not about transforming people's character so that they stop sinning and live morally upright lives in everyday practice. In fact, God justifies *sinners*, people whose character and lifestyle deserve a verdict of condemnation. He is not unjust in declaring us righteous, because our justification is based on something other than our performance.

Second, justification is based solely on the finished work of Christ (Rom. 3:23–26; 5:18–19). God's verdict about believers cannot be based on their own standing before God, for on their own they are justly under God's wrath and deserve eternal condemnation for their sin. But God's wrath is met by His infinite mercy in Christ. For Christ lived the perfect human life in this fallen world and was perfectly righteous and well-pleasing in the Father's sight. Christ died on the cross for our sins, fully satisfying God's wrath against our sins as the sinless sacrifice. Christ then rose again, confirming the acceptability of His sacrifice and issuing in new life for His people. By virtue of believers' union with Christ, Christ's sinless life, atoning sacrifice, and resurrection become theirs.

Third, considering what Christ has done for believers, justification has two aspects. On the one hand, Christ's sacrifice means all their sins—past, present, future—are paid in full in God's sight and they are forgiven completely (Isa. 53:6; Rom. 3:25; 2 Cor. 5:21; Eph. 1:7; 1 Peter 2:24). When people sometimes say that justification means God treats believers "just as if they never sinned," this is the aspect they are stressing. But this is only half the story, for on the other hand, Christ's perfect life means His righteousness is credited to believers (Gen. 15:6; Rom. 5:12–19; 1 Cor. 1:30; 2 Cor. 5:21; Phil. 3:9). From Christ we receive what theologians call an "alien" righteousness, a righteousness not our own, because it comes from outside ourselves. Justification therefore brings a dual imputation, a "great exchange." My sins are credited to Jesus and fully paid by Him on the cross, and His righteousness is credited to me. When the Father sees me in Christ, He not only sees me as completely cleansed of all my sin; He also looks on me with favor since I am clothed in Christ's righteousness.

Fourth, justification is received only by grace through faith (Rom. 3:21–4:12; Gal. 3:21–26; Eph. 2:8–9). It is a free gift of God. And it can only be received through faith, through trusting in Christ alone. This is why justification is not earned through our good works in any way. It is not a process by which we do good works to earn our righteousness, at which point God then declares us righteous. Instead, immediately upon trusting Christ, we are considered no longer under condemnation and righteous in God's sight.

Fifth, although justification is not in any way grounded in good works, it inevitably results in good works (Eph. 2:8–10; Titus 2:14). The one who is justified does not "continue in sin that grace may abound, for the grace that justifies us is also the grace that transforms us to become more and more like Christ in our lives (Rom. 5:20–6:23). God has a much bigger agenda than simply delivering us from hell (Rom. 8:28–30). Consequently, while no one is justified in any way by good works, good works will inevitably follow in the lives of those who have been justified. Put differently, sanctification does not lead to justification, but it does certainly result from justification.

The description of justification outlined earlier represents a definitional standard among most Protestants. Others, however, would differ. Traditional Roman Catholicism, for instance, sees justification as a process beginning with baptism and continuing throughout our lives as we become more holy in practice. It thus rejects the forensic nature of justification, merges justification and sanctification, and insists that faith and cooperating works together effect justification. Others agree that justification is forensic, comes by faith alone, and involves forgiveness of sin. But they deny that it also includes Christ's imputed righteousness, lest we lose motivation to grow in godliness. Others still embrace the standard Protestant view almost entirely, with the exception that they deny that justification will always produce good works (i.e., sanctification) in the life of the one justified. They say that if justification is really through faith alone, then it is possible for someone to be justified without any resulting change in their life. And, of course, many people and religions are *legalistic*, thinking that they can earn a right standing with God by their own good works. As we have seen, all such views fall short of the biblical presentation on justification.

Just think what justification means if you are a believer. It means that your fundamental identity is fixed securely in Christ, regardless of your failures or successes in your Christian life. It means that all sins you have committed or will commit are paid in full. It means that you do not have to carry around guilt for the past. It means that you can reject legalism once and for all because you already have His favor and do not have to earn it. All of us can indeed heartily join David's testimony to the blessedness of "the man against whom the LORD counts no iniquity" (Ps. 32:2a ESV). But there are further blessings beyond justification.

 **Spirit Baptism**

Many Christians today testify that sometime after they became believers, they experienced another amazing work of God called "baptism in the Holy Spirit." As they understand it, this work of God, subsequent to conversion, brings the believer into a new, ongoing experience of the Spirit in which they receive greater blessing and empowerment for godly living, meaningful worship, and effective ministry. It is evidenced typically by speaking in tongues. This understanding of baptism in the Spirit is held traditionally by many Pentecostal and charismatic Christians.

But other Christians have not had this experience of a dramatic second work of grace. Do these Christians have a deficient relationship with the Spirit? Are they at a significant disadvantage compared to other Christians who have had this second work? If not, how should we understand the experience of those who have experienced a dramatic work of the Spirit in their lives?

The best way to proceed is to consider what the Scripture says about baptism in the Spirit. The expression in Greek, *baptizein en pneumati*, occurs seven times in the New Testament. Four of them involve John the Baptist's prediction that Jesus will baptize His followers with the Holy Spirit (Matt. 3:11; Mark 1:8; Luke 3:16; John 1:33). Two passages in Acts (1:5; 11:16) use the expression to describe what happened on the day of Pentecost (Acts 2) when the Spirit came upon the disciples. The last passage to use the expression is 1 Corinthians 12:13: "For in one Spirit we were all baptized into one body—Jews or Greeks, slave or free—and all were made to drink of one Spirit" (ESV).

First Corinthians 12:13 makes clear that all Christians have been baptized in the Spirit; Paul's whole argument in this context hinges on this reality. This demands that baptism in the Spirit happens *at the moment* of conversion in connection with union with Christ. Yet Christ's disciples were baptized in the Spirit on the day of Pentecost, *well after* their conversion. So which is it? The Pentecostal view's solution to this dilemma is to distinguish baptism *by* the Spirit in 1 Corinthians 12:13 from baptism *in* the Spirit in the other texts. The former happens at conversion and is true for all believers; the latter is the second work of grace described above. But this distinction has no basis in the Greek text; the same expression, *baptizein en pneumati*, is used in all seven passages. This suggests it is the same baptism in the Spirit in each text, and so it must occur at conversion.

But if Spirit baptism occurs at conversion, how do we account for the experience of Jesus' disciples on the day of Pentecost, when they were baptized in the Spirit well after their conversion? To answer that, we need to keep two important considerations in mind. First, Jesus inaugurated the new-covenant age. This included a more powerful, intimate relationship between the Spirit and each new-covenant believer than that experienced by old-covenant believers (Jer. 31:31–34; Ezek. 36:26–27; Num. 11:29; Joel 2:28–32; Acts 2). The day of Pentecost and the coming of the Spirit marked the beginning of the Spirit's new-covenant relationship with believers (Acts 2:14–21). Second, Jesus' disciples lived during the transition to this new-covenant relationship with believers. Therefore, while they believed in Jesus long before the day of Pentecost, they did not receive this new relationship with the Spirit in Spirit baptism until the day of Pentecost. But unlike believers in Acts during this transitional stage, all believers since then receive baptism in the Spirit at their conversion, as taught in 1 Corinthians 12:13.

What, then, is involved in this baptism in the Spirit that all believers receive at conversion? First, believers receive the Spirit into their lives forever thereafter (Acts 2:38; 8:14–17; 19:1–7; Rom. 8:9–11; Gal. 3:2–3). It ushers in the Spirit's indwelling (see **The Works of the Holy Spirit**), which forms the basis for all His works in believers' lives. Believers are thus initiated by Spirit baptism into the permanent, intimate relationship with the Spirit described by the new covenant. Second, while Jesus baptizes us in the Spirit (John 1:33), it is also true that through the Spirit received at Spirit baptism we experience the presence of Christ in our lives (Rom. 8:9–11). Third, baptism in the Spirit also unites the believer with the body of Christ (1 Cor. 12:13). There is a real spiritual unity in the body of Christ, and this is due to the work of the Spirit in uniting each of us to all Christians universally. One cannot be part of Christ's universal church without having the Spirit.

If all believers have been baptized in the Spirit at conversion, what might we say about those who have experienced a "second work of grace"? We need not dismiss the reality of powerful manifestations of the Spirit in the lives of believers after their conversion, even though such manifestations are not Spirit baptism as described above. Recall our earlier discussion in chapter 5 of Spirit filling, which is the Spirit's work of empowering believers beyond their own capacity. This work of the Spirit best explains the powerful manifestations of the Spirit that are often mistaken for baptism in the Spirit.

The ongoing presence of Christ and the Spirit in believers' lives, effected in Spirit baptism, is absolutely central for their growth as Christians, a topic to which we now turn.

35 Sanctification

Election, regeneration, union with Christ, adoption, justification, Spirit baptism—it can all sound so heady, so triumphal. But the Christian's day-to-day experience often feels the opposite, as we find ourselves struggling with sin in our lives. We resonate with the description of believers this side of glory as simultaneously saint and sinner. As believers in Christ, our status and relationship with the Father, Son, and Spirit are secure, and our future glory is assured. But in the meantime, we battle with sin, falling into our old patterns rather than living out our true identity in Christ. Yet this time of battle with sin is not simply a gap in God's work of salvation, an oversight in His otherwise perfect plan. It is an important part of what God is doing in believers' lives. We call this phase of God's saving work "sanctification." Sanctification is the process in which the believer is set apart from sin to Christlikeness. If justification is about legally declaring believers righteous through Christ's righteousness, sanctification is about making them righteous in their actual lives.

Biblically speaking, there are three phases of sanctification. It begins with *positional* (or *objective*) *sanctification* (Acts 20:32; 26:18; 1 Cor. 6:11). By being united with Christ at conversion, the believer is fundamentally set apart in holiness to God. For this reason, believers are called saints—holy ones (e.g., 1 Cor. 1:2; Eph. 1:1; Phil. 1:1; Col. 1:2). To be sure, believers are already holy in God's sight because we are justified. But positional sanctification focuses on the reality that believers from the beginning have been changed in regeneration (Titus 3:5; 1 John 3:9) and freed from sin's dominating power (Rom. 6). The sanctification begun at positional sanctification continues as believers become increasingly more Christlike throughout their lives, though never perfectly. This is called *progressive* (or *subjective*) *sanctification* (Rom. 6:12–13, 19; 12:1–2; 2 Cor. 3:18; Phil. 3:12–14; Col. 3:9–10; Heb. 12:1, 14). The process of sanctification is completed when all vestiges of sin are removed from believers and they are made completely like Christ at His return. This is called *final* (or *perfected*) *sanctification* (Rom. 8:28–30; 1 John 3:2).

Most discussions of sanctification focus on progressive sanctification, since this is the phase of sanctification that pertains to our Christian life this side of heaven. Progressive sanctification has five significant features. The first is that its goal is Christlikeness (Rom. 8:28–30; Eph. 4:13; 1 John 3:2). Sometimes Christians think sanctification is simply about outwardly conforming to a set of rules, as if this constitutes holiness. God's agenda in our lives is far grander than that. He wants to make us like His Son, holy and righteous from the inside out, including thoughts, attitudes, and motivations as well as actions.

Another feature of progressive sanctification is that it is, as its name indicates, a progressive work. Scripture uses several images like growth (1 Peter 2:2; Eph. 4:11–16), a race (Heb. 12:1–4), or a battle (Eph. 6:10–20) to describe it. The expectation is that the longer we are Christians, the more we grow in maturity toward Christlikeness (Rom. 6:19; Heb. 5:11–6:3; Eph. 4:11–16). Yet we must remember that the process of growth will never be completed in this life; we will not be conformed fully to Christ until final sanctification. Some Christians, however, deny this, claiming that it is possible to achieve sinless perfection in this life. But the New Testament teaches that indwelling sin will continue to remain in us this side of heaven (1 John 1:8–10; 3:2; Rom. 6; Gal. 5:16–25).

A third feature of progressive sanctification is that it is God who sanctifies us in Christ (1 Thess. 5:23; 1 Cor. 1:30; John 15:1–5). In particular, we are sanctified by the Holy Spirit (2 Thess. 2:13; Gal. 5:16–25). We are not able to change ourselves; only God can do that. By His grace, He "has granted to us all things that pertain to life and godliness" (2 Peter 1:3 ESV). For this reason, some Christians argue that the Christian's role in sanctification is purely passive. They maintain that we should "let go and let God" sanctify us by getting out of the Spirit's way in His sanctifying work; our own efforts in our sanctification are fruitless exercises in self-dependence. This view rightly recognizes that only God can sanctify us, and that we must always firmly rest in His gracious provision and entrust ourselves to Him in order to grow (Rom. 6:13, 19; 12:1–2). But it fails to take into account the active role given to believers in the New Testament for their sanctification.

This leads to a fourth feature of progressive sanctification. Believers must cooperate with God's sanctifying work in their lives. As we have just seen, Peter declares that God has given us all the provision we need for spiritual growth (2 Peter 1:3–4)—but then he immediately tells us "to make every effort" to grow in godliness in light of this provision (vv. 5–11). Similarly, speaking of our sanctification, Paul tells us in Philippians 2:12–13 ESV to "work out your own salvation with fear and trembling"—but then why this is possible: "for it is God who works in you, both to will and to work for his good pleasure" (ESV). Indeed, Scripture repeatedly exhorts Christians to grow in godliness in light of divine provision (e.g., Heb. 12:14; Rom. 8:13; 1 Cor. 6:18; 2 Cor. 7:1; 1 Thess. 4:3; 2 Tim. 2:22).

But how do we cooperate with God's sanctifying provision? Here we come to a fifth feature of progressive sanctification. Believers must avail themselves of various gracious means that the Spirit uses to sanctify us. We should not think of these as mechanistic processes that force the Spirit's hand whenever we practice them. Instead, they are our regular practices that He graciously uses to help us grow. In fact, we should not expect to grow if we forsake these means. But they must always be accompanied by trust in God's power and provision to sanctify us, lest we fall into the trap of thinking we are sanctifying ourselves. These means include prayer (Acts 2:42; Eph. 6:18; Phil. 4:6–7), worship (Acts 2:42; Eph. 5:18–20), reading and meditating on Scripture (John 17:17; 2 Tim. 3:16–17; Heb. 4:12), active obedience (Gal. 5:16–25; John 15:10), self-discipline and denial (Titus 2:12; 1 Cor. 9:24–27), endurance in suffering (James 1:2–4; Rom. 5:3–5), and true fellowship with other believers in the church (Acts 2:42; Eph. 4:11–16; Heb. 10:24–25).

The wise Christian will not treat progressive sanctification as if it were optional. Those who seek to grow in godliness glorify God in their lives (Matt. 5:16); help others to grow (Eph. 4:11–16); experience blessings in this life, such as the fruit of the Spirit (Gal. 5:22–23); and anticipate pleasing their Master when they meet Him face to face (2 Cor. 5:9–10; Rom. 14:10–12). Those who profess to know Christ but forsake progressive sanctification give evidence that they really do not know the Lord they claim (1 John 2:3–6; Rom. 6:1–2). True believers—imperfect, sinful, frequently failing though they may be—continue to fight sin in their lives until Christ calls them home. The next term explores this more.

36   Perseverance of the Saints

Most of us know people who once professed to be believers, but then fell away from Christ. Maybe they embraced a sinful lifestyle at odds with the Christian faith. Maybe they became angry with God, other professing Christians, or the institutional church. Maybe they found atheism or another religion more appealing. Maybe they simply lost interest in the Christian faith. But whatever the cause, these formerly professing Christians no longer follow Christ, and may not even identify themselves as Christian anymore.

What has happened to people like this? How do we understand what's going on in their lives? To answer those questions, we need to consider whether it's possible for true believers to *lose their salvation*. Many Arminians—particularly those in the Wesleyan tradition—affirm that it is. They believe one's final salvation is conditioned on whether the believer continues to cooperate with God's saving grace. If genuine believers persist in willful sin or abandon the faith altogether, they forfeit the blessings of salvation they once had. Advocates of this view appeal to passages in Scripture which exhort believers to persevere and warn them about falling away (e.g., Rom. 11:22; Col. 1:21–23; Heb. 6:4–6).

In contrast to conditional salvation, many others—Calvinists in particular—insist that salvation, once given by God, is unconditional. They hold to *eternal security*, the doctrine that the final salvation of all genuine believers is guaranteed because it is secured by God's power. This view is supported by repeated promises of Scripture that the believer's salvation is secure (e.g., John 10:27–30; 2 Tim. 1:12; Rom. 8:28–39; 1 Peter 1:3–5). Passages like this teach, as Peter puts it, that true believers have "an inheritance that is imperishable, undefiled, and unfading, kept in heaven for you, who by God's power are being guarded through faith for a salvation ready to be revealed in the last time" (1 Peter 1:4–5 ESV). Little wonder that Paul declares that nothing can "separate us from the love of God in Christ Jesus our Lord" (Rom. 8:38–39 ESV).

If we accept the eternal-security position, we must consider another question. How do we know who is a genuine believer? The answer can be found in a doctrine closely related to eternal security: the perseverance of the saints. This doctrine maintains that the true believer will persevere in their faith by God's power until their final salvation (John 8:31–32; Phil. 1:6; 1 Peter 1:5; Heb. 3:14; Jude 21, 24). If eternal security stresses that it is God who ensures our final salvation, perseverance of the saints reminds us that we are not passive but responsibly participate (by His power) in what God has guaranteed. It follows from perseverance, then, that those professing Christians who do not persevere demonstrate that they were never truly saved in the first place; they had a false faith. This is the key to understanding the warnings and exhortations cited by advocates of conditional salvation. These texts serve to distinguish merely professing believers from genuine believers who heed the exhortations to persevere.

In its definition of perseverance, the Westminster Confession (17.1) says: "They, whom God hath accepted in His Beloved, effectually called and sanctified by His Spirit, can *neither totally nor finally* fall away from the state of grace; but shall certainly persevere therein to the end, and be eternally saved" (emphasis added). It goes on to say (17.3) that a true believer might neglect "the means of their preservation, fall into grievous sins; and, for a time, continue therein: whereby they incur God's displeasure, and grieve His Holy Spirit." This nuanced statement of perseverance rightly points out that a true believer might enter into temporary periods of serious sin or doubt (Matt. 26:70–74; Eph. 4:30; Mark 16:14; 1 Cor. 11:32). Yet such backsliding is indeed temporary, for a true believer will return to the Lord and endure to the end (Matt. 10:22–23; 24:12–13; Rev. 2:7).

But how do we know the difference between a true believer who backslides for a time and a professing Christian who was never truly saved? To answer this question, we must address the topic of *assurance of salvation*. This is the believer's personal confidence of being genuinely saved and guaranteed of final salvation. It is important to bear in mind that assurance involves a person's subjective state, not necessarily his or her objective condition. That is, a genuine believer may lack assurance; or conversely, a person confident of salvation may lack true saving faith. Scripture indicates that the Lord wants His children to experience assurance (1 John 5:13; Rom. 8:16; cf. Heb. 11:1).

Why, then, do genuine believers sometimes lack assurance of salvation? It may be due to a lack of knowledge of God's Word and promises. It may be brought on by life's trials and difficulties, raising questions about whether God truly loves the one experiencing these difficulties. It may be caused by slipping into legalistic thinking, basing assurance on one's good performance rather than on the finished work of Christ. It may be driven simply by a disposition to doubt. And there may be other reasons as well. How we minister to those lacking assurance will take different forms depending on the cause (Jude 22).

But there is another factor that will likely lead to lack of assurance: a lifestyle of persistent sin in a professing believer's life. And this *should* cause doubt, because such a pattern is inconsistent with what it means to be a Christian (1 John 3:9). This means that, from our perspective, we may not be able to tell the difference between a true believer who is backsliding and a professing believer who was never truly saved in the first place. But in either case our response should be the same: gospel proclamation. Backsliding believers need to live a life consistent with the gospel, and false believers need to truly receive the gospel for the first time in their lives.

Genuine believers have good reason to persevere in the faith. True, we face trials, battles with sin, troubles in a sin-cursed world, and oppression and persecution by the forces of evil. But the sufferings of the present time cannot compare with the glory that will be ours in Christ when He returns (Rom. 8:18). Let's consider that future glory more closely.

37 > Glorification

We all love those times when we find ourselves pleasantly surprised by something that exceeds our expectations. Those times give us a glimpse of the Christian's eternal future, for no matter what we might say about it, our final destiny will be beyond what we can imagine this side of heaven. Paul put it this way in 1 Corinthians 2:9: "No eye has seen, no ear has heard, and no mind has imagined what God has prepared for those who love him" (NLT). Still, even though we can only glimpse our future in a fragmentary way, reflecting on that future is well worth the effort.

The Christian's final destiny in Christ is called glorification. This is the final stage in God's work of salvation when the believer is fully sanctified, conformed to the image of Christ, and given an immortal, resurrected body like Christ's glorified body. Scripture describes several elements of glorification. First of all, our bodies will be resurrected, and they will be transformed into a glorious body like Christ's resurrected body that will endure forever (Rom. 8:22–25; Phil. 3:20–21; 1 Cor. 15; 2 Cor. 5:1–5). To those of us whose bodies are aged, weak, painful, disabled, or sickly, the thought of a body forever free from all such infirmities is unspeakably good news (see **Resurrection**).

In addition to resurrection, at glorification we will be fully conformed to the image of Christ (Rom. 8:29–30; 1 John

3:2–3). This includes our resurrection, of course, but beyond that, it means that all vestiges of sin will be eliminated from our lives once and for all. No more struggles with besetting sins; no more falling to temptation; no more struggles with evil thoughts, wrong motives, and sinful attitudes; no more coming short of what God wants for us. In Christ, final deliverance from sin in all its forms and effects will be ours; our final sanctification will be realized. And because Christ is the true image of God and pattern for redeemed humanity (2 Cor. 4:4; Rom. 5–6), we will be completely restored to all that God intended human beings to be when He created us.

Believers' glorification will also include full participation and fellowship with the perfected people of God. All God's people, individually and corporately, will be perfected in holiness (Eph. 5:25–27; Rev. 19:6–8). Together as one we will worship the Lord (Rev. 7:9–10). We will enjoy full citizenship in the heavenly city with all God's people (Phil. 3:20; Heb. 11:8–16; 13:14; Rev. 21:9–22; 22:5). We will together rejoice in the perfect realization of God's eternal rule and will serve Him and reign with Him forever in the new heaven and earth (Rev. 7:15; 22:3–5).

Perhaps greatest of all, our glorification will include unhindered fellowship with the triune God (Rev. 21:1–4, 22–27). Spiritual death—that alienation and hostility to God introduced at the fall—will be forever reversed. The intimate fellowship with God enjoyed by our first parents will be restored, and more. This is the heart of eternal life (John 17:3).

Our moments of joy in worship in the present are only pale glimpses of the bliss of unhindered fellowship with the living God. It is this for which we were made; it is this for which the human heart longs, whether it realizes it or not. David says of God that in His presence there is "fullness of joy" and "pleasures forevermore" (Ps. 16:11 ESV). When we are glorified, that joy will be ours, because God will be ours.

9

THE DOCTRINE OF THE CHURCH

(Ecclesiology)

38 ➤➤ The Church

Grab your phone and find the last full-family picture you have. What resemblances do you see? Is it in the color of your eyes, your shared height (or lack of it), or a certain distinguishing facial feature? Usually there is some shared physical characteristic that hints toward a family relationship—a way to know you belong to that particular kin group and not another. What about in our membership in the family of God? What distinguishes the church as the body of Christ from other socioreligious groups? To answer that question, we need to highlight some of the "family resemblances" found in Scripture.

The word we use for "church" comes from the Greek term *ekklēsia*, which is used in Matthew 16:18 when Jesus says to

Peter, "Upon this rock I will build My church; and the gates of Hades will not overpower it" (NASB). The term *ekklēsia* can refer to a civic decision-making group, an ad hoc gathering of people, or a group formed because of shared beliefs. The biblical context must be studied to determine which meaning is intended, but generally you will see it translated as "church," "congregation," or "assembly." The theological significance of its use, however, is a different matter.

The church is an elect assembly of people who are in Christ and thus part of His body through baptism in the Holy Spirit. This includes the *universal* or *invisible church*—all those who have put their faith in Christ between the day of Pentecost and Christ's return, whether they are now in heaven or still on earth (Acts 2:41; 15:14; 1 Cor. 12:12–13; Eph. 1:3–6, 22–23; 4:4; Col. 1:18; 1 Thess. 4:16–18). It also includes the *local*/singular or *visible*/trans-regional church(es), which is a Christ-present assembly of baptized Christ followers, submitted to the authority of Scripture, whose mission is to preach and proclaim the gospel and to practice rightly the ordinances of baptism and the Lord's Supper. They have organized themselves for mission and evangelism, edification and worship, hospitality and fellowship, in the context of the spiritual gifts of their members (Acts 2:41–47; Matt. 18:20; 28:19–20; Rom. 16:15; 1 Cor. 4:17; 16:19; Gal. 1:22; Philemon 2).

Identifying the authentic local or visible church has proven a challenge throughout church history. One important way to discern family resemblance is through a historic confession articulated in the Nicene-Constantinopolitan Creed of AD 381, which affirms our belief in "one, holy, catholic, and apostolic church." Reformers such as Martin Luther and John Calvin expanded on these, focusing on the preaching of the gospel and the correct performance of the sacraments; later, the Belgic Confession (1561) added church discipline to the marks. Evangelicals further developed their understanding of these as well, including a more robust understanding of mission, worship, and hospitality.

The four original *marks of the church*—one, holy, catholic, and apostolic—are still important family characteristics that remind us of the global, intergenerational family to which we belong. Believing in "one" church highlights our unity based on our shared membership in the body of Christ (1 Cor. 12:12–18), of which He is the head (Eph. 4:15–16). Holding to the "holy" or set-apart nature of the church reminds us that we are God's temple and the location of His presence (1 Cor. 3:16). His presence dwells in us and calls us to lives of holiness together in community (1 Cor. 6:19; Eph. 5:26–27). Affirming the "catholic" mark, or the universality of the church, reminds us of the shared connection with Jesus for membership. He is the vine and we are the branches (John 15:1–8); He is the shepherd and we are the sheep (John 10:14–15). John 10:16 reminds us of the diverse nature of the universal church, while Jesus' prayer in John 17:21 calls us to a proper ecumenism—a global movement that promotes unity among true churches while still recognizing diverse expressions and understandings of following Christ (a challenge indeed!). Finally, holding to the "apostolic" mark—or better, the apostolic writings—reminds us of the centrality of the Scriptures to our family portrait. While Peter is the focus in Matthew 16:18, other accounts, such as Ephesians 2:20, broaden the persons involved in the foundation of the church: "the apostles and prophets, with Christ Jesus himself as the chief cornerstone" (see also Heb. 2:3b–4). It is important to be clear on the definition of the church. Why? So that we will be able to discern faithful expressions of the body of Christ in the world today.

39 Israel and the Church

Looking again at our church-family picture, an important question arises: Is Israel in it? Your answer will depend on what you mean by "Israel." Israel refers to the Jewish nation, God's historic and continuing covenantal people. It includes the land and the state of Israel today. The church in the new covenant is distinct from Israel in the old covenant. The church has not replaced Israel as God's people—that is a view known as replacement theology or supersessionism. Some theologians consider the church to have replaced ethnic Israel as God's chosen people and have become "the Israel of God" (Gal. 6:16) or the "new Israel" (a term the New Testament never uses). The reference to the "tribes of Israel" in Revelation 7:4 is thought to indicate that the church has become the spiritual Israel (Rom. 9:6–7; 11:17–21). However, Romans 11:29 (NASB) asserts, "The gifts and calling of God are irrevocable." Paul argues in Romans 9–11 that God's covenant relationship with Israel has not ended (Rom. 9:6; 1 Cor. 7:17–24). When the New Testament uses the term "Israel," it refers to historic, ethnic Israel and not to the church. This does not mean that the church is not closely identified with Israel; in Ephesians 2:11–12, Paul reminds in-Christ Gentiles they are part of the "commonwealth of Israel" (ESV). Their Gentile congregations are satellite communities of Israel, in a manner similar to the way member countries of the British Commonwealth were part of the United Kingdom while maintaining their unique national identity. In that way, our church-family picture would be incomplete without God's people Israel, for our identities are interrelated (Rom. 15:10, 27).

It is best to keep the referent for "Israel" as the "children of Israel," the physical descendants of the patriarch Jacob, whose name was changed to Israel in Genesis 32:28 (2 Kings 17:34). In Genesis 35:10–11, Jacob's name change is narrated again, but this time it's promised that "a nation and a company of nations shall come from you" (ESV). The phrase "children of Israel" only occurs four times (1 Kings 6:13; Isa. 17:3, 9; Rom. 9:27 KJV), but is evident in other English expressions such as "Israelites" (Ex. 1:12; Heb. 11:22), "sons of Israel" (Ex. 1:1), and "people of Israel" (Jer. 50:4; Rev. 2:14).

Israel is a key self-referential term used by the descendants of Jacob. It functions as insider language describing those who have been chosen by God. It also indicates a focus on covenantal identity for those who are part of God's people through Jacob/Israel. Other terms for this group include "the Hebrews" (Ex. 1:22; Phil. 3:5) and "the Jews," though the latter term develops later and connects the people of Israel to the land of Judea (Ezra 6:14; Neh. 1:2; 1 Cor. 1:22). The church is a distinct entity from Israel in God's economy, and confusing these terms will create theological confusion and can lead to supersessionism, a crucial ethical concern in our post-Shoah—after the Holocaust—context.

Supersessionism refers to the theological position that once Christ came and established the church, the new-covenant community replaced the nation of Israel as God's chosen people—and thus Israel's covenantal relationship and identity as such ceased. It occurs among theologians and pastors in three ways. First, the Bible's full story is read in such a way that Israel's story does not continue, or is insignificant once we reach the New Testament. This gets to the heart of the problem, namely hermeneutics (see **Theological Hermeneutics**). Second, Israel's rejection of Jesus in the first century results in an expression of God's retributive justice and a turning to the church as the new Israel. Third, Israel functions as a literary foil, a salvation-historical necessity whose role in prefiguring Christ was accomplished and is now obsolete. Here typological interpretive methods are often used as, for example, baptism replaces circumcision as the covenant sign (Col. 2:11–12).

A *post-supersessionist* theological method includes the following hermeneutical presuppositions and practices: (1) God's continuing covenantal faithfulness to Israel; (2) Jesus is the eternal second person of the Trinity and the Messiah of Israel; (3) the gospel is for all people, both Jews and non-Jews; (4) Gentiles who come to faith in Jesus are part of God's family without needing to become Jews; and (5) Messianic Jews, as part of their membership in Israel, should continue to identify as Jews, reflecting Israel's call to be a separate and abiding nation. This is not a two-covenant approach to salvation, one for Jews (i.e., Torah) and one for Gentiles (i.e., Jesus). But it does see the canon as an unfolding narrative, rather than assuming the earlier stories are obliterated by the later ones.

Post-supersessionism also seeks to systematize theology in a way that doesn't imply a revocation of God's covenant with the Jewish people. It pays close attention to the Jewish nature of the Bible and suggests an Israel-centered hermeneutic that should complement Christ-centered and gospel-centered ones. A post-supersessionist theological position, as an advancement on progressive dispensationalism, attempts to interpret the primary teachings of Christian theology and church tradition in a manner that doesn't suggest the discontinuance of Jewish covenantal identity. This also matters because getting Israel's identity right can help us navigate other identity-based problems in our contemporary culture, as we uncover God's desires for human embodiment in its spiritual and physical dimensions.

40 Baptism

Many evangelicals in the United States think that Christian baptism occurs when a believer is immersed in water in the Trinitarian name of the Father, Son, and Holy Spirit. It is seen as a public testimony and symbol of the person's prior acceptance of the gospel. It occurs after their profession of faith in the completed work of Christ, and it functions as the initiatory rite into the local or visible church. This is referred to as *believer's baptism*. Matthew 28:19–20 is central for this doctrine: "Therefore go and make disciples of all nations, baptizing them in the name of the Father and of the Son and of the Holy Spirit, and teaching them to obey everything I have commanded you. And surely I am with you always, to the very end of the age." This text highlights that one first must be a follower of Jesus—a disciple—before baptism should occur. The public-identification aspect is implied in the public nature of the rite, along with the invocation of the Trinitarian formula. The initiatory aspect is assumed from the person's embrace of the teaching or catechizing ministry of the church.

Nearly every part of this definition has been debated in

church history, and this continues among evangelicals today. In regard to the *mode* or the particular way of baptizing, some churches practice sprinkling, or even effusion or pouring, rather than immersion. Most agree that baptism is the initiatory rite into the church but disagree if this is reserved for believers (*credobaptists*), or if it can properly be practiced on infants (*paedobaptists*). Others question if baptism is only a symbol; they instead see it as a means of grace. Still others extend this to the point where they teach that it effects a saving work of the Holy Spirit; this is known as *baptismal regeneration*. While it is important to come to a reasoned biblical-theological conclusion on the theology and practice of baptism, we ought to expect diversity in regard to this rite and to practice hermeneutical hospitality toward those who differ.

Two additional terms relate to one's view of both baptism and the Lord's Supper. Some writers prefer the term *sacrament*, which has come, following Augustine, to mean a visible sign of an invisible grace. Among evangelicals, these sacraments are seen as effective only when accompanied by God's Word and faith. (It isn't seen as effective only by the act itself, as in the Roman Catholic sacramental system.) Others, seeking to distance themselves from such sacramental approaches, prefer the term *ordinance*, since it doesn't include the idea that the rite conveys grace; it is only a symbol. Often those using the term "ordinance" do so since they conclude that Christ ordained baptism (Matt. 28:18–20) and the Lord's Supper (Matt. 26:26–29). So, these terms may be used synonymously in practice; however, they do represent two differing approaches to baptism and the Lord's Supper.

Immersion is the most appropriate mode for baptism. The Greek word for "baptize" (*baptizō*) in differing contexts in the New Testament can mean to dip, immerse, or plunge in water. This seems to be what occurred in Jesus' baptism (Matt. 3:16), as well as the Ethiopian eunuch's baptism by Phillip (Acts 8:38–39). Immersion also best symbolizes the believer's identification with Jesus' death, burial, and resurrection (Rom. 6:3–5; 1 Cor. 15:3–4; Col. 2:12).

Those who support sprinkling as the primary mode do so by noting that immersion would have been improbable in several locations (Acts 2:41; 8:38; 16:33). This at least suggests more than one practice at this early stage (Heb. 6:2a). The typological connections warrant sprinkling rather than immersion (Ex. 24:6–7; Lev. 14:7; Heb. 9:10). The lexical support for *baptizō* tends toward circularity.

Still others see effusion or pouring as the preferred mode. Pouring out seems most appropriate to the eschatological ministry of the Holy Spirit (Acts 2:17–18). The prepositional phrases in Jesus' baptism, as well as the Ethiopian eunuch's baptism, can be understood to reflect pouring rather than immersion (see also *Didache* 7:1–4). The scenes from the catacombs in Rome offer early evidence of diversity of practice in regard to baptism.

Believers are the most appropriate candidates for baptism in light of Matthew 28:19. Acts 2:38 further substantiates this as Peter instructs those desiring salvation to be baptized subsequent to their repentance. The broader context of Acts 2:38–47 also highlights these baptized believers as becoming members of the Christ-group. It also makes sense in light of the way salvation washes away sins and removes God's judgment (Acts 22:16; 1 Peter 3:20–21).

The infant-baptism position is undergirded by the idea that baptism is a sign of the covenant. Support for this is partly based on Colossians 2:11–12, which typologically links circumcision with baptism. Infants under the old covenant were circumcised, so it follows that under the new covenant infants should be baptized. If this typological relationship holds, then it is likely infant baptisms were practiced in the New Testament era.

There is some evidence of early Christian baptism of infants in Origen and Cyprian, and in the catacombs, though the practice didn't become widespread until the late fourth or early fifth centuries. The household context is also an important argument for the paedobaptism position. The passage most often pointed to is 1 Corinthians 7:14, since it highlights the idea that the children of a believing household are considered "holy." There are several clear examples of household baptisms in the New Testament more broadly (Acts 16:5, 30–31; 18:8; 1 Cor. 1:16). It is important to note that both sides of this debate have scriptural support for their positions. Worshiping only as Scripture prescribes is crucial for those in Reformed churches (see **Worship**), so it is unlikely they would not seek to support their position from Scripture.

Ultimately, it is important to listen with open-minded humility to those who differ on this issue. This doctrine matters since it is the initiatory rite into the church, and we need to be clear on what we think about it. But it also matters as a good test case for the way we practice unity amid diversity within the body of Christ.

41 The Lord's Supper

While baptism is the initiatory rite into the church, the Lord's Supper is the continuing rite. It is an ordinance, since it was ordained by the Lord during His last supper (Matt. 26:26–29; Luke 22:19) and so should be practiced until His second coming (1 Cor. 11:26). It's also referred to as "Communion" or the "Eucharist," and some churches see it as a sacrament rather than an ordinance. It involves several symbolic elements: the broken bread is symbolic of Jesus' broken body; the wine, for His shed blood that provided atonement for sin (1 Cor. 11:23–25). When received among the church it symbolizes the participants' reception of Christ's work as our substitute. It also symbolizes gospel proclamation, for Paul wrote, "For whenever you eat this bread and drink this cup, you proclaim the Lord's death until he comes" (1 Cor. 11:26). The corporate act is the declaration. It also involves social memory—"do this in remembrance of me" (1 Cor. 11:24)—

reinforcing the group's identity and unity as those in union with Christ. And it is an ongoing reminder that the church is a new-covenant reality: "This cup is the new covenant in my blood" (1 Cor. 11:25b).

The new covenant is a relationship promised to Israel, the framework by which the nation would be governed during the future messianic kingdom (Jer. 31:31). By God's grace the church participates in some of the blessings of this covenant, based on Christ's work on the cross (Matt. 26:28; Ex. 24:8), though complete realization awaits

WHILE BAPTISM IS THE INITIATORY RITE INTO THE CHURCH, THE LORD'S SUPPER IS THE CONTINUING RITE.

in the future. A person has a right relationship with God through Christ only on the basis of the new covenant (Heb. 9:18–20). Paul understands himself to be a minister of the new covenant (2 Cor. 3:6), a covenant that is salient in the present era in a non-supersessionist way. God has enlarged the scope of the blessings of the covenant but that does not change the way in which He will fulfill His covenant promises to Israel. He has done more, not less, than He promised. Practicing the Lord's Supper reminds us of God's covenant faithfulness to Israel and to nations.

Jesus' words in 1 Corinthians 11:24–25, "This is my body"—and a similar expression concerning His "blood"—has been the focus of theologians and pastors throughout church history (Matt. 26:26, 28). What did Jesus mean by "is"? The Roman Catholic Church teaches that the elements of the Mass are changed into the literal body and blood of Christ. They become mystically present when the priest pronounces the consecration formula over the bread and wine. This is referred to as *transubstantiation* and is rejected by Protestants. The Lutheran theological position contends that the person partakes of the true body of Christ in, with, and under the elements (*Formula of Concord*, 7:35). There is no actual transformation of the elements, as in the Roman Catholic view. This is referred to as *consubstantiation*: Christ's real presence is there in, with, and under the bread and wine.

The *spiritual-presence* view, in contrast to the two real-presence views, contends that Christ is spiritually present through the agency of the Holy Spirit and the elements manifest His presence. This is the view found in Reformed, Calvinist, and Presbyterian churches. The Lord's Supper is more than a mere symbol or memorial; it is a means of grace.

The fourth view, the *memorial* one, goes back to Swiss Reformer Huldrych Zwingli (1484–1531), who recognized "is" as a figure of speech, signifying or symbolizing Christ's body and blood. This view is evident among Baptistic, Bible, and free churches. It is symbolic, similar to the eating and drinking in John 6:53–54 and the non-means-of-grace sharing in 1 Corinthians 10:16. Partaking in the Lord's Supper is still a testimony of one's faith (Heb. 9:22) and a public acknowledgment of a new identity (Heb. 10:20). The elements symbolize

Jesus' pierced body (John 19:33, 36) and His suffering and death (Matt. 20:22). The focus for the memorial view is the Lord's Supper is to be done in remembrance of Jesus.

Who may participate in the Lord's Supper has been a question throughout church history. The first prerequisite is that a person needs to be in Christ. This is often referred to as regenerate participation—only those born again by the Holy Spirit may partake (John 3:3–8; James 1:18). Fellowship with Christ and other believers will not occur simply by the act itself. Those who are in Christ but out of fellowship with other believers in a local congregation may be prohibited from participating. Historically, self-examination and confession of sin have been key parts of preparing to rightly take the Lord's Supper (1 Cor. 11:27–32; cf. Ps. 66:18; 1 John 1:8–9).

Reflection on participation in the Lord's Supper also extends to one's ecclesial identity. Often, in traditions that refer to it as "communion," you will come across "open" communion, "closed" communion, or "close" communion. The *open* perspective allows anyone in Christ to participate; and since this tradition understands it as an ordinance of the universal church, anyone may administer it. It may also be taken in diverse locations and not limited to the church gathering.

The *closed* view contends that only members of a particular church may participate. The administration of the table is strictly regulated and it may only be taken under the auspices of a local church. The Roman Catholic Church is the foremost example of this view.

Finally, the *close* understanding holds that those in a right relationship with God and part of a local church may participate in the ordinance. The table is still regulated by a local church. In terms of who may be permitted to administer it, and while it does vary, there is still a preference for the Lord's Supper to occur during the congregational service.

As we can see, the meal that was designed to unify those in Christ has often been the occasion to divide them. Maybe we can appreciate the diverse ways in which churches have understood the Lord's Supper as a gift rather than a problem to solve. Maybe rediscovering the meaning of the Lord's Supper can allow us to develop a spirit of hospitality and *koinōnia*, the communal life together we have in the triune God with one another (1 Cor. 1:9; 10:16–17; 2 Cor. 13:14).

42 Church Leaders

Who's in charge here? Who's supposed to lead this church? Such questions show how practical theology can be, as it offers answers to these commonly asked questions. There are two offices in a local church: (a) elder/overseer/pastor and (b) deacon. The first group administers oversight of the church, while the second group serves the church. In the New Testament an *elder* (*presbyteros*) is generally synonymous with an *overseer* (*episkopos*) or a *pastor* (*poimēn*), although the post-apostolic church made distinctions between the terms. This variation has led some denominations to make a distinction between an elder and an overseer, often referred to in English as a bishop. The qualifications for an elder may be found in 1 Timothy 3:1–7 and Titus 1:5–9. The primary responsibilities of an elder/overseer/pastor include teaching (1 Tim. 3:2), guarding against false teaching (Titus 1:9), leading (1 Tim. 5:17), praying (James 5:4), and shepherding (Acts 20:28). In the Reformed tradition, there is often a distinction made between ruling and teaching elders, based on 1 Timothy 5:17. Ruling elders largely engage in administrative tasks while teaching elders largely minister God's Word to the congregation.

How many elders should a local church have? Scripture does not address that issue directly, though some guidance can be offered. There appears to have been, in some locations, multiple "elders" (*presbyteroi*). This built on existing Jewish religious leadership structures (Ex. 19:7; Mark 11:27). In Acts, we see elders being appointed in congregations including in Jerusalem (Acts 14:23; 21:18). These elders led local Christ-groups along with the apostles (Acts 16:4). There is, however, also evidence of a single-elder leadership structure as well (2 John 1; 3 John 1), though the overwhelming pattern is the multiple-elder structure. There are no examples in the New Testament of women being referred to as elders/overseers/pastors, though the boundaries evident in 1 Timothy 5:17–22 and Titus 1:5–6 would exclude some men from those positions as well.

In the contemporary debate over the role of women in church leadership, complementarianism and egalitarianism serve as the dominant options. *Complementarianism* is the theological term that describes those who hold that women and men are complementary to each other in nature, though with differing roles in both the home and the church. In regard to church leadership, complementarians contend that women are not eligible for the position of elder. Support for this comes from 1 Timothy 2:12: "But I do not allow a woman to teach or exercise authority over a man, but to remain quiet" (NASB). Additionally, the condition that an elder be the "husband of one wife" (1 Tim. 3:2) can only be fulfilled by a man. Complementarians support women serving in various ministries in a local church, with one exception—elder/overseer/pastor.

Egalitarianism is the opposing perspective; it contends that women and men are equal in both nature and roles. In the home, a husband and a wife submit mutually to one another, and in the church women and men serve side by side in all areas, including elder/overseer/pastor. Egalitarians thus resist those who identify restrictions on women in regard to church leadership. They support their position from Galatians 3:28, claiming that, in Christ, gender distinctions have been obliterated: "There is neither Jew nor Greek, there is neither slave nor free man, there is neither male nor female; for you are all one in Christ Jesus" (NASB). Since these differences have been erased, egalitarians contend, the complementarian position falters. Moreover, there are examples of women leaders in Romans 16:1–16 doing what 1 Timothy 2:8–15 claims to restrict.

Deacons (*diakonoi*) are those who serve the church and function via delegated authority from the elders and a local church. It is to be distinguished from the office of the elder, though many churches conflate the two. In the New Testament, they are seen as leaders in the earliest Christ-movement and are evident throughout. It is difficult to discern when this leadership label shifted from a generic "servant" or "minister" to a "deacon" in the official way it's used in most ecclesial settings. The influence of Jesus' teaching in Mark 10:43 likely contributed to the role and office of the deacon. The serving aspect evident in Jesus' teaching emerges in Acts 6:2–3, where the "servant" is one who waits on tables. This passage may be the point where the shift from function to office begins. Paul refers to himself and Apollos as "servants" (1 Cor. 3:5) and to himself (and others) as "ministers of a new covenant" (2 Cor. 3:6). If Acts 6 is a starting point for the institutional development of the office, then the Corinthian correspondence reflects at least the idea of servility but possibly more.

Philippians 1:1 seems to be the place where Paul uses "bishops" (*episkopoi*) and "deacons" (*diakonoi*) in ways approximating church officers. In 1 Timothy the office is more explicit, and the local congregation is given specific guidelines for the position's qualifications (1 Tim. 3:8–13). Similar to overseers, people serving in this capacity must have significant managerial capabilities and be above reproach morally; however, teaching and leading functions are not evident for them.

Women serving as elders/overseers/pastors is not evident in the New Testament. Romans 16:1, however, refers to Phoebe as a "deacon" (*diakonos*) of the "congregation" (*ekklēsia*) in Cenchrea. The question is whether this is a functional role or a Christ-movement office. It is likely that what is evident here is similar to Philippians 1:1, where some sort of office is in view. Moreover, while the term "deacon" is used primarily for men, 1 Timothy 3:11 may be understood to include a mixed-gender grouping of deacons (though some think what's evident here is only deacons' wives).

BEING CLEAR ON THE ISSUE OF LEADERSHIP IN THE CHURCH IS CRUCIAL IN ORDER TO AVOID CONFUSION AND CONFLICT.

Being clear on the issue of leadership in the church is crucial in order to avoid confusion and conflict. There are cultural and contextual reasons for diverse practices, but it's wise to closely follow scriptural guidance when it comes to these issues. In our present cultural moment, when there is significant confusion in regard to gender and authority, the need for theologically reasoned but empathically communicated biblical wisdom is of the upmost importance. Being clear on our definitions is a good start.

Worship

Worship wars. Just the mention of those two words brings back bad memories of US church life in the 1980s, even into the present time. The desire for cultural relevance and commercialization created a perfect storm when it came to incorporating new music and artistic styles in the public gatherings. Ian Malcolm, the intrepid mathematician in *Jurassic Park*, reminded the scientists in that story—and I'm paraphrasing here—that just because you could do something doesn't mean you should. Applying that question to worship-service debates may have helped us avoid some unfortunate worship-practice developments.

What does God want when it comes to worship? He tells us His desire in John 4:23–24: "Yet a time is coming and has now come when the true worshipers will worship the Father in the Spirit and in truth, for they are the kind of worshipers the Father seeks. God is spirit, and his worshipers must worship in the Spirit and in truth." What does it mean to worship "in the Spirit"? It means to worship through the empowerment of the Holy Spirit by virtue of our union with Christ. What does it mean to worship "in truth"? It indicates that the Father desires worship informed by the prescriptions found in Scripture. Notice He desires both Spirit and truth—not just one or the other.

Worship is ascribing worth, majesty, and glory to God as an expression of our identity in Christ, in line with the prescriptions of Scriptures through the Spirit's empowerment (Ps. 96:8; Isa. 6:1–8; Phil. 3:3; Eph. 2:18; Col. 3:15–17). This occurs on the personal level as we pray and offer songs of thanksgiving and praise. However, the primary area of concern is the worship gathering—when a local church comes together for their weekly service. This corporate gathering of the family of God should ascribe worth, majesty, and glory to God through singing, praying, reading Scripture, and preaching the gospel. Responses should include giving money, confessing sin, encouraging others through testimonies, and sending forth missionaries. The proper administration of baptism and the Lord's Supper should also occur. There are still plenty of opportunities to develop worship practices sensitive to one's cultural setting, but this core provides an integral starting point for a Spirit-empowered worship of God in the manner He desires. This results in a fully Trinitarian approach to worship. But this raises the question: How do we determine the manner in which we embody this? This is where the regulative and the normative principle can help.

There are two principles in regard to public worship in the church, and while some traditions, such as the Reformed, make explicit use of these guidelines, they are present in all expressions of Christianity—even if they do not use these terms. The *regulative principle* states that a public worship gathering should only include what Scripture explicitly enjoins, while the *normative principle* supports the idea that diverse practices may be included in a worship service as long as Scripture does not explicitly forbid them. Some try to offer a middle-of-the-road principle: the normative principle that does not squeeze out the regulative aspects. This approach maintains a close adherence to Scripture in terms of worship practices, but then allows for more diversity in relation to cultural practices and new expressions in the public gathering. Indeed, much of the debate over church leadership and the ordinances seen in these entries on the church reveal an underlying perspective on this issue.

The key ideas concerning what should be included in a public worship service, from a regulative-principle perspective, include the following. First, God knows best how He desires to be worshiped (John 4:24). Second, Scripture provides for us all that we need for determining the orderly and appropriate way God desires to be worshiped (1 Cor. 11:2–16; 14:26–40). Third, in light of these two ideas, only what Scripture explicitly warrants the church to do should be part of the public gathering. If there is no explicit text for a practice, then it is not to be included.

The basic concepts for the normative principle include the following. First, God knows best the way worship should be designed. Second, in light of this, God regulates certain aspects of the worship service, but He leaves significant components of the service to the discretion of the local church. These would be areas of indifference. Third, the local church has the freedom to decide in these matters, though it cannot go against Scripture. Fourth, there is no need for an explicit biblical command for a worship practice; it's permissible unless it's forbidden.

Why does this matter? If you've attended more than a couple of churches in your Christian experience, you're likely aware that what we are describing as the normative principle of worship has become the dominant position among evangelicals in the United States. Many worship services are organized without considering the scriptural basis for its practices, or even if a practice may go against a scriptural command. The suggestion here, then, is that the normative approach to worship—so long as it doesn't neglect biblical prescriptions whereby God reveals the way He wants to be worshiped—is a better way forward. Getting this definition right matters if we want to be God-centered in our worship—which hopefully we do.

I like to tell my students that if their study of theology doesn't form them into better worshipers, then I've failed as their teacher. Hopefully, one practical outcome of learning more about these fifty important theological terms is that you as well will be a better worshiper: "Therefore, since we are receiving a kingdom that cannot be shaken, let us be thankful, and so worship God acceptably with reverence and awe" (Heb. 12:28).

10

THE DOCTRINE
OF THE LAST THINGS
(Eschatology)

 The Intermediate State

People often joke that you cannot escape two things in life: death and taxes. This truism might bring a wry smile to our face during tax season, but when we stand grieving at the graveside of a loved one or friend, it is no longer amusing. Funerals have a way of sobering us. After all, they confront us with the harsh reality not only that we're finally separated from our loved one in this life, but that our own physical death is inevitable. Like taxes, death too is inescapable.

The Bible's teaching on death sobers us all the more. It confirms that *physical death* will come to everyone, and it tells us why. Adam's sin in the garden brought death into the world as God's just judgment (Gen. 2:16–17; 3:19; Rom. 5:12). Yet as terrible as physical death may be, it is not even the worst of it. We are also born *spiritually dead*, alienated from God (Rom. 8:6–7; Eph. 2:1–5) and enslaved to sin's corrupting power (Rom. 5:21–6:23). If not reversed, spiritual death leads inexorably to *eternal death*, permanent separation from God in the never-ending lake of fire (Rev. 20:14; 21:8, 27).

Yet the Bible speaks hope in the face of such grim prospects, for in Christ death has already been defeated; and when He returns, He will crush it forever (1 Cor. 15:23–26, 54–55; Rev. 20:14; 21:4). As a result, those who trust in Christ are no longer alienated from God (spiritually dead) but are reconciled to Him in Christ (spiritually alive; cf. Eph. 2:1–4). Having been delivered from spiritual death, believers will never face eternal death; they will instead enjoy the bliss of unending fellowship with the Lord (Rev. 21–22). And even the sober reality that believers will continue to face physical death until Christ returns is mingled with hope. For Christ promises that at His return He will resurrect our dead bodies and transform them into a body like His own resurrected body—glorious, powerful, and imperishable (1 Cor. 15:42–44). Physical death too will be defeated in the end (see **Resurrection**).

IN CHRIST, WE ARE ALREADY FIT FOR HEAVEN.

This is all good news indeed, but it also raises an inevitable question people naturally ask at funerals. If resurrection awaits Christ's return, where is my loved one *now*? Put differently, what happens to people between their physical death and their bodily resurrection at Christ's return? This period of time is called the intermediate state.

What does Scripture teach about this? Let's start with what it does *not* teach. Some incorrectly claim that most believers (except the holiest few) go to *purgatory* when they die. Purgatory is a place of suffering where the souls of believers are gradually purged of their remaining sins until they are fit to enter heaven. But Scripture nowhere teaches that such a place exists. Further, a believer has no sins needing to be purged after death. The believer's sins have been paid in full by Christ's atoning work on the cross (Rom. 3:21–26), and there is "now no condemnation for those who are in Christ Jesus" (Rom. 8:1). In Christ, we are already fit for heaven.

Others mistakenly describe the intermediate state of believers as *soul sleep*. In this view, after death the souls of believers continue in *unconscious* existence, only to reawaken to consciousness when their bodies are raised at the resurrection. Although it appeals to Scripture's speaking of death as "sleep" (e.g., Matt. 9:24; John 11:11–14; 1 Cor. 15), this view misunderstands biblical teaching. The point of the metaphor is not that believers lose consciousness in the intermediate state but that physical death for them is no more permanent than sleep. Further, as we will see, Scripture teaches that the intermediate state is a time of enriched fellowship with Christ "away from the body," rather than a dormant state without consciousness.

According to the Bible, then, what is the intermediate state like for the believer? The souls of believers continue to exist apart from their bodies, which remain behind and decay (Phil. 1:23–24; 2 Cor. 5:4, 8) until they are raised again at Christ's return (1 Cor. 15). Instead of suffering in purgatory, our souls go to be "with" Christ in heaven (Phil. 1:23), where we will be "at home with the Lord" (2 Cor. 5:6, 8). Because we will not experience soul sleep but will be able to interact with others in the intermediate state (see Luke 16:19–31; Rev. 6:9–11), we will enjoy enriched fellowship with Christ. This is why the intermediate state can be seen as desirable and "far better" (Phil. 1:23) than our current condition. Still, the intermediate state falls short of perfection, for only at Christ's return will we be "clothed" with our resurrected body (2 Cor. 5:1–5).

Scripture teaches that there is also an intermediate state for nonbelievers, but their prospects are not as sanguine. The central biblical text is the story of the rich man and Lazarus in Luke 16 (especially vv. 22–26). On his death, the body of the condemned rich man is buried, but his soul is sent to *Hades*. He's clearly conscious of his dire straits there. It is a place of torment, far removed from the blessed existence of the saints in heaven. Hades is not yet the final destination for the condemned; eventually, it will lead to eternal death in the lake of fire at the final judgment (Rev. 20:11–15).

A biblical perspective gives believers hope in the face of physical death. Christ has defeated death; it has been "swallowed up in victory" (1 Cor. 15:54). Grievously evil though it may be, physical death nevertheless ushers us into the presence of the Lord, a desirable state that is better by far (Phil. 1:23).

Believers therefore need not be terrified of death, and their sorrow over it will always be mingled with hope (1 Thess. 4:13). Sadly, the same cannot be said for nonbelievers, as physical death ends any hope for escaping inevitable judgment. These destinies are certain, and the next term confirms why.

The Second Coming of Christ

Christians are a people of hope (Heb. 11:1; 1 Cor. 13:13; 15:58), and for good reason. We look forward to the Second Coming of Christ—His bodily return to earth in glory and triumph. When He returns, Christ will complete His grand work of redemption, mete out final justice, restore all creation, dwell forever in fellowship with His renewed people, and more. No wonder Paul declares that the growing Christian waits eagerly "for our blessed hope, the appearing of the glory of our great God and Savior Jesus Christ" (Titus 2:13 ESV). When Christians lose sight of this gloriously sure future, they lose heart or become foolishly distracted by the allures of this world. The wise Christian, then, will frequently reflect on this wonderful future.

What will Christ's return be like? He is going to come back personally (John 14:3; Acts 1:11; 1 Thess. 4:16), physically (Acts 1:11; Rev. 1:7), and visibly (Rev. 1:7; Matt. 24:30–31).

Even though there will be signs anticipating His return (Matt. 24), His coming will be sudden and unexpected in the world (Matt. 24:37; 25:1–13; 1 Thess. 5:2–3; 2 Peter 3:3–4). It is of no use to try to set dates for His return—as far too many have tried to do—because no one knows when He will return except God Himself (Matt. 24:36; 25:13; Mark 13:32–33). In fact, we should always be watching and ready for His return, because His return is *imminent*—it could happen at any time (Matt. 24:42–44, 50; Luke 12:40; James 5:7–9; Rev. 1:3; 22:7). (See **The Rapture** to consider how the imminence of Christ's return fits with the signs of His return.)

Christ's second coming involves a complex series of events and their aftermath. This complexity leads to a variety of theological positions regarding His return (which we will revisit later in this chapter). But Protestant evangelicals do agree on some basic realities about His return. We agree that Christ will return literally to the earth and that as a result He will finally vanquish all the forces of evil, fully realize His kingdom reign, raise our bodies from the dead, effect final judgment, and usher in the eternal states of the believer and nonbeliever.

Still, there are significant differences as well. We disagree about whether Christ's second coming will be a single event, or whether it will occur in two phases, a rapture and then His return to earth. We disagree over the nature of Christ's kingdom reign, the millennium. We disagree over whether the nation of Israel has a specific role in His kingdom reign (see **Dispensationalism**). We disagree over whether there will be a great tribulation—a time of unprecedented evil and judgment—prior to the realization of Christ's reign on the earth. We disagree over the timing of the resurrection and judgment. All these differences warrant separate entries of their own in this chapter. So too does the matter of heaven and hell, the eternal states of the believer and nonbeliever. Let's look more closely at these issues, and in so doing, better understand the second coming of Christ.

46 The Millennium

Disagreements about the when and how of Christ's second coming begin with the millennium. This refers to the 1,000-year period taught in Revelation 20:1–10, during which Christ reigns with His saints on the earth. There are three basic millennial views, and they differ on the nature of the millennium and whether Christ returns to the earth before or after it. What are these millennial positions?

Amillennialism maintains that Christ's millennial rule began with His resurrection and ascension and thus we are currently in the millennium. The millennium is not a literal 1,000-year reign of Christ from the earth over the earth; it is an indefinitely long period of time in which He reigns spiritually from heaven over the church. The millennium will end some-time in the future when Christ returns to the earth. At that time there will be a general resurrection of all human beings and then the final judgment, ushering in the eternal states.

Postmillennialism is structured just like amillennialism, since in both views Christ comes back after the millennium. The major difference between amillennialism and postmillennialism is the nature of the millennium. Granted, in both views Christ reigns from heaven. But in postmillennialism, His reign is not a spiritual reign alone, and the full manifestation of the millennium still remains in our future. Christ's rule over the earth grows gradually as the gospel expands to the ends of the earth and triumphs. This expansion of Christ's rule through the exponential growth of believers ushers in a golden age where evil is mitigated and the world prospers. Righteousness will triumph throughout the world, shaping culture, politics, economics, and society as a whole, as well as spiritual life. At the end of His triumphal reign over the earth from heaven, Christ will return.

Unlike the other two views, *premillennialism* maintains that Christ comes before the millennium, and He establishes it Himself. Before He returns to the earth to rule, there is a period (usually understood to be seven years) of intense evil and suffering on the earth known as the *great tribulation*. This period is identified with Daniel's seventieth "week" (a seven-year period) in Daniel 9:24–27. It is a terrible time in which satanic forces, led by the Antichrist (or the "beast" in Revelation) and his henchman (the false prophet), dominate the world and persecute God's people, while at the same time God pours His wrath on the world. Christ Himself ends the great tribulation when He returns, crushes the forces of evil arrayed against Him, and imprisons Satan (Rev. 19:11–20:3). At this point, Christ resurrects believers martyred during the great tribulation (Rev. 20:4–5); this is called the "first resurrection." Premillennialists disagree about whether at this point all other believers are resurrected as well, or whether Christ resurrects other believers in an earlier rapture (see **The Rapture**).

With His resurrected saints, Christ rules over the whole world for 1,000 years, a golden age of unprecedented blessing, peace, prosperity, justice, and righteousness (Rev. 20:4–6). Still, the millennium falls short of the perfection of the new heaven and earth, for there are those living under Christ's rule who have a rebellious heart. This is revealed when Satan is released from his imprisonment for a short time and rallies a vast multitude of rebels to take up arms against Christ, but this rebellion is easily vanquished (Rev. 20:7–10). At this point comes the final judgment, including the resurrection of unbelievers to eternal condemnation.

ALL DISPENSATIONALISTS ARE PREMILLENNIAL, ALTHOUGH NOT ALL PREMILLENNIALISTS ARE DISPENSATIONAL.

A significant number of premillennialists are dispensationalists. As we saw in the first chapter, dispensationalism maintains that the Lord made promises to the nation of Israel

in the Old Testament. Because Israel and the church are distinct entities, the church cannot fulfill those promises, and
so they remain unfulfilled. Dispensationalists teach that the
Lord will fulfill those promises to Israel during the millennium, when Israel turns to the Messiah and is redeemed. All
dispensationalists are therefore premillennial, although not
all premillennialists are dispensational.

Clearly premillennialism (in its various versions) is more
complex than both amillennialism and postmillennialism. But
its complexity arises directly from the narrative flow of Revelation 19:11–20:10, read rather straightforwardly. Because
amillennialists believe the New Testament teaches a simpler
end of history than that posited by premillennialists (e.g., in 2
Peter 3:10–13), they approach Revelation 19–20 less chrono-
logically and more symbolically. Similarly, postmillennialists
also approach this text more symbolically, believing that postmillennialism is supported by several kingdom parables that
speak of the kingdom gradually growing until it permeates the
world (e.g., the mustard seed and leaven in Matt. 13:31–33).
Premillennialists insist that a straightforward, chronological
reading of Revelation 19–20 is warranted by the text itself, as
well as by a plain reading of many Old Testament predictions
about the future.

But perhaps none of these views matters all that much
in the end. Perhaps we should just adopt a "panmillennial"
view, that it will all pan out in the end. While it might make
us feel better to dismiss a contentious issue as unimportant

and impractical, it is unwise. Apart from directly affecting how we interpret texts like Revelation 19–20, one's view on the millennium also shapes how one understands the end of the Bible's storyline. This in turn affects how one understands the entire storyline, other predictive passages, and the relationship between the Old Testament and New Testament. The question of the millennium should not be quickly dismissed. Nor should the next issue.

47 > The Rapture

Among premillennialists, there is another debate related to Christ's second coming which focuses on the question of the rapture. This refers to the event predicted in 1 Thessalonians 4:13–18 when believers—both dead and living at the time—are "caught up . . . in the clouds to meet the Lord in the air" (v. 17). Premillennialists debate whether the rapture is a distinguishable phase of Christ's second coming—and if it is, when it happens in relation to the great tribulation. The two most common views on the rapture today are the posttribulational and pretribulational views, but there are others as well.

The *posttribulational view* does not believe that the rapture is a distinguishable phase of Christ's second coming. As a result, the church will suffer through the great tribulation, and then Christ will return. When He does, all believers will be resurrected, rise to meet Him in the clouds, and immediately return with Him to earth as He defeats the wicked and establishes His millennial kingdom. Posttribulationalists maintain that Scripture nowhere teaches that Christ will come in two phases but assumes a single event; the other views are built on unwarranted inferences from the text.

Pretribulationalism asserts that the rapture will occur before the great tribulation, and then Christ will return to earth after the great tribulation to set up His millennial kingdom. Hence, Christ comes in two phases: *for* His saints before the great tribulation (rapture), and *with* His saints after the great tribulation (return to earth). The pretribulational view is typically held by dispensationalists.

Pretribulationalists make several arguments to support this view, but we will only mention two here. The first pertains to the purpose of the great tribulation. Its purpose is not only to pour God's wrath on the rebellious human world, but also to prepare Israel through trials to receive the Messiah (e.g., Dan. 9:24–27; Jer. 30:7; Rev. 7). The church has no role in either purpose. Indeed, Scripture teaches that while the church certainly should expect trials, she is exempt from the coming divine wrath related to the great tribulation (Rev. 3:10; 1 Thess. 1:10; 5:9). The second argument relates to a tension in Christ's second coming. On the one hand, Scripture teaches the *imminence* of Christ's return; He could come back at any time and so believers must be ready (e.g., James 5:7–9; 1 Thess. 1:10; Phil. 3:20–21; Titus 2:13; Rev. 22:20). On the other hand,

Scripture indicates there will be signs before Christ's return (Matt. 24). The pretribulational rapture handles this tension well: the rapture is imminent, but the signs pertain to Christ's return to earth after the rapture and tribulation.

There have been other, less common views on the rapture. All share the pretribulational conviction that the rapture is a distinguishable phase of Christ's second coming, but they differ from pretribulationalism and from one another on the timing of the rapture. *Midtribulationalists* maintain that the rapture occurs at the midway point of the great tribulation, which helps explain why Scripture mentions or alludes to this midway point several times (e.g., Dan. 7:25; 9:27; 12: 7, 11; Rev. 12:14). The *prewrath rapture* maintains that the rapture occurs three-quarters of the way through Daniel's seventieth week. The third quarter of that seven year period is the great tribulation, and so the church will suffer through that. However, the last quarter of those seven-years will be the time of God's wrath, and the church will be raptured before that (Rev. 3:10). The *partial rapture* view maintains that the rapture itself occurs in multiple phases throughout the great tribulation depending on whether the person is spiritually mature and thus prepared for Christ's coming.

Our view on the rapture has an impact on our outlook. If the rapture is imminent, we should always be prepared for His coming and await it with joyful anticipation, for He could even come today. If the rapture awaits some or all of the great tribulation, we should expect the possibility of greater suffering before Christ returns to end it forever. Since hope is so important in the Christian life (Heb. 11:1; 1 Cor. 13:13; 15:58), this is not an insignificant consideration. Neither is the next term.

48 Resurrection

It was common in the ancient Greco-Roman world to view the physical body with some disdain. What mattered most was one's spirit; the flesh was insignificant, even evil. This attitude infected some of the Corinthian believers, and Paul would have none of it. In 1 Corinthians 15, Paul makes the case for Christ's bodily resurrection, and He does so in order to insist on the future resurrection of believers' bodies as well. After all, God created us from the beginning with bodies and souls, and He declared his original creation very good (Gen. 1–2). He will redeem us in full, and that includes our bodies. This is why the intermediate state described earlier is just that: intermediate. Only when Christ returns will our bodies be raised forever.

As we saw previously, although they differ on its timing, all the views on the millennium and rapture agree that Christ's second coming will usher in the resurrection. In fact, Scripture clearly teaches that the bodies of *all* humans, believer and unbeliever alike, will be resurrected (John 5:28–29; Acts 24:15; Dan. 12:2). We know very little about the nature of the unbeliever's resurrection, except that it will be a "resurrection of judgment" (John 5:29 NASB) that inexorably culminates in the second death (Rev. 20:5–6, 13–15). Scripture focuses attention on the resurrection of believers.

Christ will raise what remains of believers' earthly bodies and transform them into bodies patterned after His own resurrected body (1 Cor. 15:22–23). What will the believer's resurrected body be like? It will be imperishable, no longer subject to sickness, disease, aging, or decay (1 Cor. 15:42). It will be glorious, both flawless and beautiful to behold (1 Cor. 15:43). It will be powerful, no longer subject to our present weaknesses but enabled to do all that God calls us to do (1 Cor. 15:43). It will be a "spiritual body," completely dominated by the Holy Spirit and no longer put to the service of sin (1 Cor. 15:44). By "spiritual," Paul does not mean non-physical, for he stresses throughout 1 Corinthians 15 that our resurrected bodies will be physical, as is Jesus'. In short, our resurrected body will be perfectly suited for living forever in the eternal state, the new heaven and earth. The resurrection of believers marks the completion of God's redeeming work in their lives, when they will finally be conformed to the image of Christ (Rom. 8:23, 28–30).

When you next go to the doctor for an illness, or look in the mirror with disappointment, or feel too tired to keep moving, or struggle with physical pain, or find yourself changing for the worse with age, or keep falling into the same sinful pattern, consider: this state of affairs is not permanent. It will not always be this way. Jesus is coming back, and everything will change when He resurrects our bodies. We thus have very good reason to be "steadfast, immovable, always abounding in the work of the Lord, knowing that in the Lord your labor is not in vain" (1 Cor. 15:58 ESV). The reality of the doctrine discussed next only strengthens that motivation.

49 Judgment

When people are abused or mistreated, they cry out for justice. But true justice in this world rarely comes quickly. Sometimes it never comes at all, and the abuser may actually prosper. Even if justice does come, it is often not adequate. Worse still, sometimes those who experience injustice then turn around and mete it out to others. This world is terribly unjust, and so many people long for something better.

There will be something better. When Christ returns, He will come to judge (Matt. 25:31–46; Acts 10:42). He will do so with perfect justice (Isa. 11:3–5; Rom. 2:11–12; Rev. 19:1–2), and nothing will escape His purview. It is a reality to inspire both hope and dread—depending on one's relationship with the Judge (2 Thess. 1:5–10).

Who will be judged? Christ will judge all unbelievers (Rev. 20:11–15). No one will have any legitimate defense against His righteous judgments, and so all will be condemned (Rom. 3:19) to eternal punishment in the lake of fire (Rev. 20:13–15). Nevertheless, there will be degrees of punishment meted out based on how unbelievers have lived (Matt. 11:22, 24; Luke 20:47; Matt. 12:36). In addition, Christ will judge fallen angels, including Satan (2 Peter 2:4; Jude 6; Rev. 20:10). This too will result in just, eternal condemnation. Remarkably, Scripture indicates that believers will participate with Him in some of this judgment (1 Cor. 6:2–3; Rev. 20:4), although it is not clear how—and in any case, we only do so by virtue of our union with Christ.

Christ will also judge believers (2 Cor. 5:10; Rom. 14:10, 12). This judgment is sometimes called the *bema judgment* (or the judgment seat of Christ; Rom. 14:10; 2 Cor. 5:10). In the Roman world, the *bema* was a raised platform from which a judge decided a case or officials issued athletic rewards. Notably, this judgment does not threaten our eternal life at all, for there is no condemnation for those in Christ Jesus (Rom. 8:1; John 3:16–18; 5:24). Instead, it will evaluate believers' works (1 Cor. 3:12–15), including their faithfulness (1 Cor. 4:1–2) and hidden motives (1 Cor. 4:5). This judgment results in different degrees of reward for the believer (2 Cor. 5:10; 1 Cor. 3:15; Luke 19:11–27).

As with the resurrection, the various eschatological views may differ on the timing of the judgment. Most of the views maintain that all judgment takes place right before the eternal states (cf. Rev. 20:11–15). However, many dispensationalists maintain that there are several phases of judgment: (1) the *bema* judgment of believers after the rapture; (2) a *judgment of the nations* after the tribulation and before the millennium, to determine who can enter the millennial kingdom; and (3) the *great white throne judgment* at the end of the millennium, resulting in the final judgment of all unbelievers. But whether in phases or a single event, all agree that Christ will indeed come as perfect Judge over all. This gives believers ample reason to faithfully serve Him, share the gospel with those facing condemnation, and trust Him to make all things right in the end. It also results in the final condition of all human beings, to which we now turn.

50 — The Eternal States

Where is history going? This profound question is one every worldview must answer. The Christian answer, found in Scripture, is clear: the doctrine of the eternal states (or final states). As the name indicates, this describes the eternal condition of all human beings resulting from the consummation of God's work of redemption and judgment. There are two eternal states, that of the condemned (hell) and that of the redeemed (heaven).

Let's start with the bad news, the eternal state of the condemned. Those who have never been redeemed by Christ through faith in Him (and are thus still in their sins) face *hell* as their inevitable destiny (John 3:18, 36). The term "hell" encompasses both the intermediate state of unbelievers in Hades and their final state in the *lake of fire* (*Gehenna*). The focus here is on the latter. The fundamental reality of the final state of all unbelievers is eternal death, banishment forever from the living God and the infinite joy His presence entails. Instead, they face the dreadful prospects of God's holy wrath (Rom. 2:6–8; 5:9; 1 Thess. 1:10; 2 Thess. 1:7–10; Rev. 6:15–18; 9:15), "a terrifying thing" indeed (Heb. 10:31 NASB). It is a place of ruin and suffering, being described as "eternal fire," (Matt. 25:41), "destruction" (Matt. 7:13–14; 2 Thess. 1:9), "outer darkness" where there will be "weeping and gnashing of teeth" (Matt. 8:12), and torment "with fire and brimstone" (Rev. 14:10–11). This suffering indicates that its inhabitants will be conscious. Worse still, they will experience it eternally (Matt. 25:41, 46; Mark 9:43, 48; Rev. 14:9–11; 2 Thess. 1:9).

The reality of hell reflects God's just punishment, a righteous reckoning (Matt. 24:46). As a result, there will be degrees of punishment in hell (Matt. 11:21–24; Luke 12:47–48; 20:47). Yet for everyone in hell, the punishment will never end, for sin is an offense against the infinite God, calling for an infinite punishment; and in any case, it's likely that hell's inhabitants will continue to sin throughout eternity.

Because the prospects of nonbelievers are so horrifying, some try to minimize them. *Universalists* claim that eventually all human beings will be reconciled to God and end up in heaven. But this violates Scripture's teaching that hell is an *eternal* reality for all unbelievers. In addition, *annihilationists* maintain that the condemned in hell will suffer for a time, but eventually they will cease to exist. They argue that Scripture's language of "destruction" and "fire" suggests annihilation, and this annihilation is "eternal" in the sense that it lasts forever. But in regard to hell, the language for "destruction" more likely speaks of ruin rather than annihilation. Moreover, Scripture's teaching about eternal *conscious suffering* militates against the notion that the condemned cease to exist. Sadly, then, Scripture does teach that the prospects of the unbeliever are as horrifying as described previously. The believer's appropriate response to the reality of hell is sorrow for those condemned (e.g., Rom. 9:2–3), awe before God's righteous judgment (Rev. 19:1–3), a passion to share the gospel with the lost (2 Tim. 2:10), and thankful praise for God's redemptive work in our lives (Rom. 11:33–36).

The prospects of believers are infinitely brighter, for *heaven* is their future. Like the word "hell," "heaven" similarly refers both to believers' intermediate state as well as their final state. Again, the focus here is on the latter. Revelation 21–22 describe the eternal state of the redeemed as a *new heaven and earth*, indeed, as the *New Jerusalem*. Sin in all its forms and effects will be forever banished, as will death itself, in this place with no sorrow, no suffering, no pain. It will be a place of unspeakable beauty, resplendent in glory—Eden intensified and expanded. We will dwell there with our glorified, immortal bodies, perfectly suited for endless life. But most important of all, God Himself will dwell there with His people, and so we will experience the unending bliss of unhindered fellowship with Him. It is this for which we were made. Little wonder that believers long for Christ's soon return. "Amen. Come, Lord Jesus" (Rev. 22:20).

ACKNOWLEDGMENTS

FROM BRIAN

I would like to say thanks to David for partnering with me on this book amid the busy life of a professor. Your theological awareness and commitments are evident throughout this book. Thank you for asking the hard questions. I would like to thank John A. Jelinek, my seminary theology professor, colleague, and friend, for encouraging me to move into theological studies as a way to bring together a lot of diverse interests and passions. Thanks Amber; Ashley and Matt, along with their twins Mason and Levi; Alexandria and John; Annaliese and Abigail. You all are a constant source of love, joy, happiness, and humor.

FROM DAVID

I am grateful to Brian for inviting me to share in this work. You are a fine scholar and a blessing to work with. I also want to thank Moody Bible Institute for the sabbatical they granted me, part of which I used for writing this book. As always, I am so very thankful for my family: my wife, Kathy, and daughters Katie, Emily, and Rebecca.

Also, I should note that significant portions of the chapter on eschatology are taken (with some adaptation) from my chapter on eschatology in *The One Volume Seminary* (Chicago: Moody Publishers, forthcoming).

FROM BRIAN AND DAVID

We are grateful to Bryan Litfin at Moody Publishers for his vision for this book. We also want to thank Matt Smethurst, our editor, for helping us clarify and simplify our words. Your professionalism and theological acumen were on target throughout the process.

THEOLOGICAL
TERMS INDEX

YOU'VE GOT BIBLE QUESTIONS.
WE'VE GOT ANSWERS.

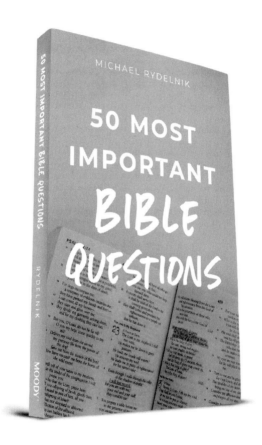

MOODY
Publishers®

From the Word to Life®

The Bible is full of great truths for our lives . . .
and a lot of mysteries that we don't understand.
But there are good answers to them all. Don't
stay in the dark any longer. Get the answers
from an expert and let your confusion turn to
understanding.

978-0-8024-2031-2 | also available as eBook and audiobook

STUDY THE BIBLE WITH PROFESSORS
FROM MOODY BIBLE INSTITUTE

MOODY
Publishers

From the Word to Life

Study the Bible with a team of 30 Moody Bible Institute professors. This in-depth, user-friendly, one-volume commentary will help you better understand and apply God's Word to all of life. Additional study helps include maps, charts, bibliographies for further reading, and a subject and Scripture index.

978-0-8024-2867-7 | also available as an eBook

WHAT SOCIAL IDENTITY CAN
TEACH US ABOUT CHURCH UNITY

MOODY
Publishers®

From the Word to Life®

Drawing from research on personal and group identity,
All Together Different equips readers to navigate
a culture that often pays lip service to the value of
diversity, but struggles to foster constructive dialogue
and mutual respect. With clear writing and real-life
stories, it translates social identity theory for pastors,
church leaders, and ministry practitioners to help their
communities work toward unity.

978-0-8024-1808-1 | also available as an eBook

ONE OF THE BESTSELLING BIBLE DICTIONARIES ON THE MARKET SINCE ITS INTRODUCTION IN 1957

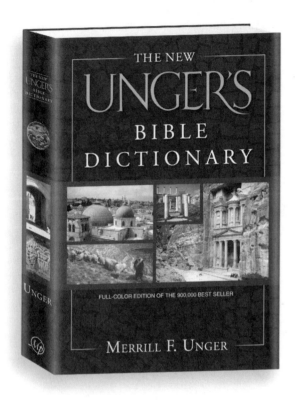

MOODY Publishers

From the Word to Life

A bestseller for almost 60 years, this time-honored classic is now more valuable than ever. Its 67,000-plus entries, reflecting the most current scholarship, are supplemented with detailed essays, colorful photography and maps, and dozens of charts and illustrations to enhance your understanding of God's Word.

978-0-8024-9066-7 | also available as an eBook